"Leroy Barber, out of the depth of his love for God and others, offers a direct, patient, and sustained critique of the failure to recognize or address issues of race or structural injustice in Christian ministry and missions. This book surfaces tensions of race that exist, but are largely ignored. They are uncomfortable, at times frustrating, and often hit too close to home. The historical detail and pastor's heart with which it is written, however, will force the reader to wrestle, repent, and reevaluate beliefs, practices, and commitments. For some it will liberate and encourage and for others it will painfully shatter illusions of reality and privilege. Don't read this for entertainment, but out of a desire to reclaim the beauty and justice of Christian missions and the hope we can more fully reflect the love of God for all his children in both the ends *and* means of justice work."

—Ken Wytsma, president of Kilns College, author of *Pursuing Justice: The Call to Live and Die for Bigger Things*

"An insightful resource for Christian leaders with a vision for multicultural communities! Drawing from a diversity of voices from the black, Asian, Latino, and First Nations communities, this book provides both practical steps, prophetic observations about culture, and historical context for the current reality of the North American church. These are insights born from a life lived in the trenches! A helpful voice for both the urban ministry setting and the broader missions community!"

—Nikki Toyama-Szeto, Senior Director of Biblical Justice at International Justice Mission, coeditor of *More than Serving Tea*

"OUCH! This is as hard-hitting a book as you will find in the annals of Christian mission literature. In your face (if you are a white male), convicting (if you are a white-led ministry), and remarkably practical (whether you are majority or minority). If you want to get serious about racial reconciliation and justice, this book will take you into the heart of the issue."

—Bob Lupton, founder of FCS Urban Ministries, author of *Toxic Charity*

"This is a hard-hitting, inspirational, challenging book that looks at the unintentional racism and arrogance in many of our Christian settings, especially in missions. Barber shares his personal experiences and the stories of others and includes some interesting historical insights. It is a book grounded in the Christian faith and Biblical frame. It opens our eyes (especially as white persons) to our mistaken ways, calls us to repentance, but most importantly challenges us to work in specific ways to change the way we work together and encourage leadership."

—Mary Nelson, President Emeritus,
Bethel New Life, Inc., Chicago

"Rev. Leroy Barber is telling the truth in this book in ways that make me weep, rejoice, and pray. Like Dr. Martin Luther King's 'Letter from a Birmingham Jail,' Rev. Barber's passionate and courageous witness has the power to change the church—if the church will receive it. All believing Christians who are committed to participate in God's mission, of all racial and ethnic backgrounds, need to read this book and pay attention."

—Rev. Alexia Salvatierra, coauthor, *Faith-Rooted Organizing*:
Mobilizing the Church in Service to the World

"In his new book, my good friend Leroy Barber exposes the need for the Church to fully embrace Biblical diversity in all of its dimensions. The integrity of our witness as agents of love, reconciliation, and justice in our world depends on our commitment to this bold vision."   —Noel Castellanos, CEO, CCDA

"More than a history and a sociological analysis of racism inherent in many missionary efforts, Leroy Barber speaks out of the hurt and disillusionments of a black man serving as a leader within ministries dominated by whites who held funding and decision making power."

—Tony Campolo, professor of sociology, Eastern University

"Let me warn you: This is not a feel-good book. It's uncomfortable and challenging but also very necessary and prophetic. In *Red, Brown, Yellow, Black, White* Leroy Barber has written a book that I believe has the capacity to impact the future of the Church and how we engage in the broad work of missions and ministries—locally and globally."

—Eugene Cho, Senior Pastor, Quest Church, author,
*Overrated: Are We More in Love with the Idea of
Changing the World Than Actually Changing the World?*

"In the daily work of our churches, para-churches, and missions agencies, it is easy to forget that the goals, systems, and structures of our work along with the demographic make-up of our organizational leadership were largely shaped by choices made decades, even centuries ago. Biblically grounded *Red, Brown, Yellow, Black, and White: Who's More Precious in God's Sight?* challenges all who lift the banner of *Missio Dei* to examine the historic and current-day choices made by culturally-bound church leadership of yesteryear. It also paints a clear picture of the real-time impact of those choices on the capacity of the church to fulfill its mission today. Leroy Barber, a long-time well-respected insider in the missions world, lifts a mirror and calls his peers to face reality. But Barber goes the distance. He offers practical tools for positive movement forward. If you like things as they are in the world of missions, then put this book down now. If you are disturbed by the disconnect between Paul's Galatians 3:28 baptismal liturgy, "There is no longer Jew or Greek, there is no longer slave or free, there is no longer male and female; for all of you are one in Christ Jesus," and the sweeping reality of the segregated ranks of church and missions leadership—if you are not afraid to face the hard truth and its implications on the mission of God in our world, then open, read and engage the re-formation of missions today."

—Lisa Sharon Harper, senior director of mobilizing at *Sojourners*,
author of *Evangelical Does Not Equal Republican...or Democrat*,
co-author *of Left, Right, and Christ: Evangelical Faith in Politics*,
and *Forgive Us: Confessions of a Compromised Faith*

ALSO BY LEROY BARBER

New Neighbor
Everyday Missions

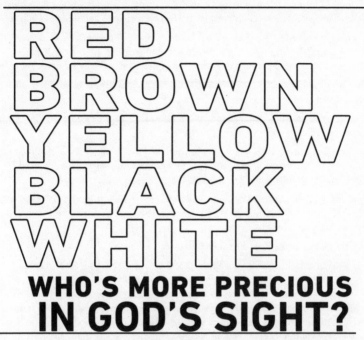

RED BROWN YELLOW BLACK WHITE

WHO'S MORE PRECIOUS IN GOD'S SIGHT?

A call for diversity in Christian missions and ministry

LEROY BARBER
WITH VELMA MAIA THOMAS

JERICHO
BOOKS

New York   Boston   Nashville

Jericho Books
Hachette Book Group
237 Park Avenue
New York, NY 10017
www.JerichoBooks.com

Printed in the United States of America

RRD-C

First edition: September 2014

10 9 8 7 6 5 4 3 2 1

Jericho Books is an imprint of Hachette Book Group, Inc.
The Jericho Books name and logo are trademarks of Hachette Book Group, Inc.

The Hachette Speakers Bureau provides a wide range of authors for speaking events. To find out more, go to www.HachetteSpeakersBureau.com or call (866) 376-6591.

The publisher is not responsible for websites (or their content) that are not owned by the publisher.

Library of Congress Cataloging-in-Publication Data

Barber, Leroy.
    Red, brown, yellow, black, white—who's more precious in God's sight? : a call for diversity in Christian missions and ministry / Leroy Barber. — First edition.
        pages cm
    ISBN 978-1-4555-7495-7 (hardcover) — ISBN 978-1-4555-7493-3 (ebook)
  1. Christianity and culture.   2. Cultural pluralism—Religious aspects—Christianity.
  3. Missions.   4. Church work.   I. Title.
    BR115.C8B365 2014
    261—dc23
                                                            2014008002

This book is dedicated to family, friends, mentors, and heroes who have gone before me. I by no means stand alone in this moment. I am part of a village that has paved the way, that still supports me in the present, and that will continue to sustain generations to come.

I gratefully acknowledge my partner in life, Donna, who is with me at all times, and our beautiful children, Jessica, Joshua, Joel, Asha, Jon. We honor our mutual mentors, Rev. Greg Johnson, Betty and Aidsand Wright-Riggins, Deacon Thornton and Frances Anderson, and many family members.

This book takes a look at diversity, and I must honor my many white, Latino, Asian, and native brothers and sisters with whom I have had the honor of journeying through hardship, tears, and joys.

Jesus Loves the Little Children

Lyrics by C. Herbert Woolston

Jesus loves the little children
All the children of the world
Red, brown, yellow
Black and white
They are precious in His sight.
Jesus loves the little children
Of the world.

Jesus died for all the children
All the children of the world
Red, brown, yellow
Black and white
They are precious in His sight.
Jesus died for all the children
Of the world.

Jesus rose for all the children
All the children of the world
Red, brown, yellow
Black and white
They are precious in His sight.
Jesus rose for all the children
Of the world.

"I've heard this [call to diversity] twenty-five different times for the last fifteen years. The book *Christian Imagination* is a great work. It's high reading; it's not for the common person. What Parnell wrote in the 1960s and rewrote in the 1990s, what coauthor Michael Emerson wrote with Christian Smith in *Divided by Faith*, and all of Tom Skinner's books made room for this book. Those books were very strong and they made a pretty good impact at that time. What they said wasn't anything new for people of color but was an epiphany for white people. I'm glad they wrote, but I don't know what really changes things. This [call to diversity] is still something we have to pray through. Hopefully this book can be an epiphany for white evangelicals today. I would argue that it will, at least, enlarge the discussion."

—*an African American missions leader*

CONTENTS

Contents

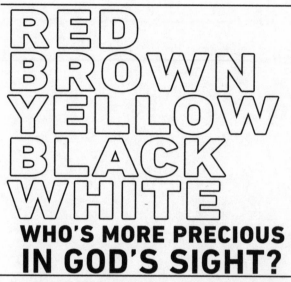

RED
BROWN
YELLOW
BLACK
WHITE

WHO'S MORE PRECIOUS
IN GOD'S SIGHT?

A call for diversity in Christian missions and ministry

PART I

THE MISSIONS MISTAKE

CHAPTER 1

Missio Dei and
Its History

"It is not the church that has a mission of salvation to fulfill in the world; it is the mission of the Son and the Spirit through the Father that includes the church."

—*Jurgen Moltmann*

"Missions is not primarily an activity of the church, but an attribute of God. God is a missionary god."

—*David J. Bosch*

The Latin term *Missio Dei* means "mission of God" or "the sending of God" in Christian theology. Missions are part of the very nature of God. The true missionary idea comes only from God.

The church exists because of the "mission of God," and the church is an active participant in the "mission of God." The church's mission is a subset of God's larger mission. Therefore, we Christians affiliated with churches, campus ministries, and other organizations are part of God's mission to the world, but we are not the entirety of God's work in the world. Each entity involved in missions is a part of the *Missio Dei*, but we must not regard our role as being identical to the *Missio Dei*. God sends whom God sends. The missions initiative comes from God.

As missionaries we have been called to represent the *Missio Dei* and must be careful how we present God's work because the repercussions of misrepresentation are too great. The mission of the Almighty is much larger than our understanding and, therefore, our culture. No one culture reflects God's mission for the world.

In missions, we share the Gospel and, implicitly, our culture. But when we insist others give up *their* culture for Christianity, we become colonizers. *Missio Dei* is not a call to culturalize and patronize nonbelievers; rather, it is delivering the Gospel without judgment or cultural bias. A decision to devote your life to missions means you agree to represent the heart of God as best you can and as accurately as you can.

Early European missionaries in Asia, Africa, and South America insisted the natives where they served abandon their culture as requisite to accepting Christ. They defined acceptable behavior and norms according to European standards. They promoted the status quo imposed by their countrymen, supported white supremacy, and benefited from European hegemony. More than being disturbed by the sin of enslaving human beings, white missionaries often viewed slavery as nothing more than an opportunity to preach to the enslaved. Colonization was the true mission, and the belief that whites were more advanced than other races was the mind-set of most missionaries. Their biases were woven into the message they shared, consciously or unconsciously. These missionaries misrepresented the *Missio Dei* through the filter of their own cultural and racial bias, and their distorted sharing of the Gospel has led to centuries of pain.

Today those biases and prejudices continue to inflict pain but in different manifestations. Contemporary efforts generally fail to build authentic relationships between whites involved in urban missions and persons of color serving God in urban communities. This absence of relationship in missions has created a system of lack. Urban missions so often lack diversity, lack multicultural expression of the Gospel, and lack depth in the delivery of service. Urban missions based on race results in white, black, Latino, and native services rather than a unified expression of the *Missio Dei*.

A further reason for the lack of diversity is because in missions organizations funded and led by whites, minorities often have neither power nor influence, even when they hold titular positions of authority. Funders, missions partners, and accountability colleagues may silently, even subconsciously, withdraw their support from leaders of color. They trust leadership that resembles them—same race, same class, same cultural background. Christians of color may earn positions of power in urban missions, but frequently they are not given backing, confidence, or latitude to make mistakes.

The true losers in this scenario are urban neighborhoods. The most effective not-for-profits (NFPs) led by indigenous people of color in urban neighborhoods targeted for missions are mostly excluded from funding. Donors feel more comfortable with white leadership and are more likely to support those with whom they relate well. Leaders of color relate well to people in the neighborhoods to be served, know more about the culture, and therefore do better work. Nevertheless, funders rarely recognize that a leader of color may be the better investment.

The Great Awakenings

The First Great Awakening (mid-1730s–1740s) had little impact on slavery. One of the most popular evangelists of the movement, George Whitefield, himself a slaveholder and a proponent of reinstatement slavery in Georgia, preached about the spirituality of slaves. Whitefield encouraged slaveholders to acknowledge the spiritual (but not earthly) freedom of the enslaved. Whitefield chastised slaveholders in the American South for mistreating the enslaved and for not attempting to convert them to Christianity. Rather than encourage those held in bondage to run away, Whitefield argued, Christian conversion would make them accept their enslaved condition. Whitefield wrote: "I challenge the whole World to produce a single Instance of a Negroe's [sic] being made a thorough Christian, and thereby made a worse Servant. It cannot be." Source: http://www.encyclopediavirginia.org/

"The more distressed and impoverished (and hence often less white) a neighborhood, the more likely organizations with white leadership are funded to work in that neighborhood than organizations composed of and led by people of color."

—*African American pastor*

_Letter_to_the_Inhabitants_of_Maryland_Virginia _North_and_South_Carolina_1740

The First Great Awakening may have stirred slave-holders to consider the idea that even black men and women had souls; however, it did not challenge the institution of slavery. This falls short of the Gospel message. While we see Whitefield's love for God coming through, we also see his fear of man hindering him from completing the message.

The Second Great Awakening (1790s–1840s) drew thousands to evangelical meetings and gave birth to powerful societies and abolitionist movements that fought to end slavery. The American Anti-Slavery Society was comprised of God-fearing men and women who advocated an immediate end to slavery. Yet slavery was deeply entrenched in the American culture, and the superiority of whites was embedded in their psyche. They used the Bible as justification for these distorted beliefs.

God wants to know us and know us deeply.

Missionaries and missions supporters who sit in church every Sunday, reducing missions to evangelism, lessen the depth of who God is and who God can be in somebody's life. These often well-meaning Christians who say they know God, but they don't know the devastation of lives—children in foster care, parents who sell their children to the sex trade, families who go hungry while seeing others dine lavishly. They want to help the less fortunate, but they don't understand that God wants to know them *and* those to whom they compare themselves more deeply. God is at work in the *Missio Dei* and is seeking to relate to both groups.

The vulnerable and outcast often feel far away from God, as if they are not together enough for God to care for them, or they are disappointed in God because of their situation. They may wonder if God even exists. Those are hard places in the soul. The truth is, God knows every person, even one with the hardest heart. What softens their hardness toward God is understanding and believing that God already knows them, cares for them, and is still kind. Their lives don't reflect that God already knows them deeply, knows the hardness in their souls, and despite their resistance wants a relationship with them in the midst of their vulnerability. Our role in missions is to bear witness to this, to acknowledge that God *prefers* to know them, and to let them know how much God loves them.

Once you are known by God, you are free. Even in human relationships, once someone knows you, you are free to be yourself. Missions that seek to change the culture of others are not freeing. Neither are missions that fail to distinguish culture from Christ. Neither are missions where those serving feel superior or more blessed by God than those whom they serve. And perhaps those who serve, well-intentioned with such attitudes, are blind to God wanting to truly know those served and to know them deeply.

This book is meant to be a tool that Christians involved in missions organizations—primarily in U.S. urban areas, but also on campuses and even in international urban settings—can use to begin a dialogue about diversity in missions leadership so that their work can truly represent the *Missio Dei*.

How did we get here? A look at missions history.

How did missions and service wind up being a place of such controversy? Why do race and racism play such dominant roles in modern-day missions? Why are we currently known more for our division and lack of heart than for our missions service? We must look back and examine the past in order to chart a new course that reflects the heart of God. In so doing, we can overcome a brutal history and create authentic ways for people to connect and serve in true partnership. If we are able to serve together despite the ugly history of missions, that alone will speak to the power of God.

To establish a foundation for missions history, we must first look at perhaps the most effective early missionary or evangelist—Saul of Tarsus, later known as the apostle Paul. He was a Jew, a Pharisee, and a freeborn Roman citizen. Moreover, he was a zealous persecutor of Jesus's early disciples. Saul had a life-changing conversion while traveling the road from Jerusalem to Damascus, bringing captured followers of Jesus from Jerusalem. Acts 9:4 tells us that suddenly there shone a light from heaven and he heard the voice of the resurrected Jesus, saying "Saul, Saul, why persecutest thou me?" (KJV).

The holy light left Saul blind for three days. While in this humble state, Saul realized the gravity of his actions and repented. He proclaimed Jesus to be the Christ and Lord with eternal dominion and power. Saul's conversion was incredible. His transformation surprised everyone else as much as it did him. Can you imagine the man who had killed your new brothers and sisters for their faith showing up at your door and professing to be a believer also? While that probably was a lot to accept, Paul, who is no longer called Saul, also begins to proclaim a message that likely was every bit as startling: God had chosen him to preach Christ to the Gentile world.

You might think that based upon his conversion, Paul would be welcomed into the fellowship of the disciples of Jesus. Not so. For Paul's tenets went against the culture and religious convictions of the Jewish believers. In reaching out to the Gentiles, Paul allowed converts to forgo circumcision and eased dietary laws and strict adherence to the Law of Moses. Paul's extension appealed to non-Jews but led to open conflict with some of the disciples. The disciples and Paul eventually parted ways, but Peter, James, and John gave Paul the "right hands of fellowship" to go and spread the Gospel. Paul took Barnabas with him and preached to the heathen (Gentiles), while the disciples preached to the circumcised (Jews) (Galatians 2:9). So began the practice of missions targeted toward different types of people. Paul's Christianity took root in Rome, the beginnings of modern-day Christianity.

I have heard this scenario used as justification for the separation of race and culture in missions and service. I cannot imagine that Paul and the early disciples envisioned missions with the magnitude of injustice, racism, and inhumanity that would follow.

Paul's willingness to not make Jewish customs a part of following Christ made the Gospel more acceptable to the non-Jewish world and allowed him to reach more people. Yet missionaries ever since have approached their converts' culture with disdain. Often the indigenous cultural practices were belittled, dismantled, or cited as a roadblock to salvation. In the missionaries' zeal to make "them" like "us," they have destroyed cultures, presumed superiority, sown mistrust, and left deep wounds.

Certainly not every missionary effort has had a sinister, underlying plot. Missionaries have done great work spreading the Gospel, building schools and churches, and providing clean water and health care. No one can take away the good that has been and is still being done. But in the effort to do good, harm has been inflicted. Thus, evangelism is regarded negatively and represents a takeover by outsiders—people who look, think, and behave differently; people who hold power, money, and influence; and thus people who rule.

History has recorded both successful and failed attempts at foreign missions. We need to look at those that failed and ask why. Likewise, we should look at the successes and gain lessons. Sprinkled throughout this book are sidebars that present capsule summaries of a broad overview of missionary work by Europeans and their impact on indigenous people. These are presented as a starting point for more research and reflection. This look into history is not meant to open old wounds, impose guilt, cause people to feel responsible for the past, or negate the progress that has been made. I do believe there has been progress. On the contrary, I mean to remind us of work still yet to do and also to inform those who may be ignorant of the painful journey that people of color have endured at the hands of missionaries working on behalf of God. History must ignite in us a desire for something better.

Age of Exploration

During the Middle Ages, Europe was an island unto itself. The Age of Exploration (fifteenth through eighteenth centuries) brought Europe face-to-face with people of color and vastly different cultures. Thus began an era of conquering people in Asia, Africa, and the Americas. There were lands to conquer, gold to pillage, people to enslave, and infidels to Christianize. While Cristóbal Colón's (Christopher Columbus's) early voyages to "America" in 1492 garnered wealth for Spain, they also resulted in enslavement and forced religious conversion on the native population.

Columbus wrote to King Ferdinand and Queen Isabella of Spain:

> "YOUR HIGHNESSES, as Catholic Christians and Princes who love the holy Christian faith, and the propagation of it, and who are enemies to the sect of Mahoma [Islam] and to all idolatries and heresies, resolved to send me, Cristóbal Colón, to the said parts of India to see the said princes...with a view that they might be converted to our holy faith..."

That Christianity and missions work are tied to difficult eras in converts' history is without dispute. Religion is tied to culture; no believer can have one without the other. Because Christianity was joined to colonization, one cannot be addressed apart from the

Source: E. G. Bourne (Ed.), *The Northmen, Columbus and Cabot, 985–1503* (New York: Mark Scribner's Sons, 1906), 90. http://www.under standingprejudice.org/nativeiq/columbus.htm

At the head of the exploration was the Catholic Church. In 1452, Pope Nicholas V issued the papal bull *Dum Diversas,* which granted Afonso V of Portugal the right to reduce any "Saracens, pagans and any other unbelievers" to hereditary slavery. The approval of slavery under these conditions was reaffirmed and extended in his Romanus Pontifex papal bull of 1455. In 1488, Pope Innocent VIII accepted the gift of one hundred slaves from Ferdinand II of Aragon and distributed those slaves to his cardinals and the Roman nobility. In 1493, Pope Alexander VI (by his perceived authority over the entire world) issued a papal decree, dividing the world outside of Europe to Portugal and Spain. Conquest and Christianity moved as a single force, destroying cultures in order to "improve them." The bloodstained sword made it clear: submit or perish—body and soul.

other. Christians (Catholics and Protestants alike), in their zeal to take the Gospel throughout the world, did so with minimal regard for the culture of those they sought to convert. Missionaries generally arrived before, with, and shortly after the people who colonized and subjugated the indigenous population while robbing their land of rich natural resources. Christians brought with them their worldview and belief that Western culture was superior and that white missionaries were needed to civilize backward, childlike people. White governments set the rules, white military enforced the rules, and white missionaries, by and large, complied with the rules. They also wrote the record and told the stories from their point of view.

There were a few exceptions. Some white missionaries sided with Native Americans and pleaded for humane treatment toward them. Missionaries and Christian abolitionists advocated for the immediate emancipation of Africans enslaved in America. The American Missionary Association opposed the colonization of Africa, returned Africans who had been held in bondage to their continent, and established schools for freedmen.

Missionaries traveled with Native Americans who were removed from their land and petitioned the U.S. government on behalf of the indigenous. Freeborn African Americans and those formerly enslaved traveled to the Caribbean islands and to West Africa to take Christianity to the indigenous, yet they did so under the watchful eyes of white-run benevolent societies. Christian physicians and surgeons participated in medical missions in China during the nineteenth and early twentieth centuries to combat the abuses of opium. These physicians established clinics and hospitals, provided training for nurses, and opened medical schools.

We honor this sacrificial missions work, but cannot ignore that missionaries stood as paternal figures—people who knew best and who rarely passed on leadership to the indigenous. For many non-white people, white missionaries have never been fully trusted and have never been forgiven for preaching a Gospel that hurt as much or more than it saved. Many people of color formed their own missionary societies or commissioned their own missionaries as a result of this mistrust.

In order to move forward progressively, forgiveness is needed but remains a difficult charge because the legacy of these degrading acts lingers. Traces of the past still manifest in the behavior of those involved in missions today; therefore, many missions organizations continue to operate in racial and cultural vacuums. We stand at a place in history, knowing what we know and with the opportunity to change. But that only happens when we acknowledge what has gone wrong.

I sometimes hear the argument that Paul and Peter went their separate ways and that served to further spread the Gospel, so why is that not our answer? Why not let whites do their missions work and let people of color do theirs? I do not believe that is God's will. Sanctioned separation will only continue the white-dominated missions heritage. Plus, resources and opportunities are diluted when we separate. Frankly speaking, most missions resources rest in the coffers of white-led organizations. Failing to unify with internal diversity will cause more hurt and misunderstandings and will fail to accomplish the *Missio Dei*. Whites will continue to have funding with few successes, and in some cases causing further harm, while indigenous people continue to have a limited range of impact.

Missions represent God's kingdom on earth. We need to grow together as Christians to get rid of the prejudice and division that our predecessors have seemingly cemented into our ethos. I reject the idea that all is lost and that recovery is impossible. We can recover. It is painful as we look at this infected area of our faith, but we cannot be healthy until we take the antibiotic of the kingdom. We have learned to live with the pain, waiting for Jesus to come back. This book is a call for unity now. I don't believe Jesus wants us to wait, but rather to follow his teachings and, imbued with God's spirit, to do this work now. So I don't want to wait. I want to please my God and fulfill my call to missions. I am tired of all these designations of black, brown, red, white, and yellow. Let's be one. Our history is tough to swallow, but the power of God is available to us. I believe we can get there.

CHAPTER 2

My *Missio Dei*

"It felt I was invisible, like my culture was not even recognized. I was not really recognized either. It was really painful and I still carry that with me."

—*Ra Mendoza*

This journey of urban missions began for me in the late 1980s. Since that time I have been a missionary, by choice and by call. God called; I said yes. What started as a venture into my vocation has taken me to rough edges of race and culture.

When I was growing up, missionaries were older ladies. Every fifth Sunday they dressed in white and positioned themselves in the front pew at our church. They were two or three special people I saw once every few years as they visited our church.

In 1989, I jumped at the opportunity to serve God differently and started my first nonprofit organization, not knowing where this road would lead. I left my job and began working full-time serving others as a missionary in the city where I lived. I knew it would be hard. I considered that my family would struggle financially. But never in my wildest imagination did I foresee that I would encounter so much misunderstanding around race and culture. Never did I envision experiencing so much resulting hurt and pain.

My wife, Donna, went through the 501(c)(3) application line by line. We submitted the required paperwork for Restoration Ministries, Inc., paid the incorporation fee, and about eight months later we received great news: We had nonprofit status! We could ask people to donate to us and their gifts would be tax deductible. We mailed letters once a month and met with family and friends to ask them to help support our missions work. I served as executive director, and we had a small board that met monthly. We were on our way.

That was the beginning of a journey that was filled with great joy and deep pain. The joy lay in the work and what we were able to accomplish. The pain was in what we learned about the Christian nonprofit world. That world did not support urban missions leaders of color—in my case, African American leaders. And while that world was already engaged in missions there, Christian organizations serving black communities lacked relationships with persons serving those communities from within.

Billy Graham and Tony Campolo

Before I went deeper into the Christian nonprofit world, I rarely heard the term *evangelical* and I certainly couldn't explain what it meant. But I soon discovered that in the Christian nonprofit world, evangelicals were the gatekeepers. Like many involved in urban missions, I volunteered in the Billy Graham Crusade and became immersed in Tony Campolo's Evangelical Association for the Promotion of Education (EAPE), organizations run by two of the world's most renowned evangelicals. What was made most obvious to me through my involvement was that these were white-dominated organizations that brought a lot of white people into the urban community. They had so much power and such vast resources! Billy Graham's Crusade rented Philadelphia's Veterans Stadium. Who does that without "bank"? To me, *evangelical* meant white folks who loved Jesus *and* had power and money.

Black folks involved in urban missions loved Jesus, too, but had very little power and even less money. My journey into the world of missions had begun completely from God's call on my life. I had responded because God requested, and I owed God my life. I had a wife, children, and very few resources, but I also had a "knowing" that I was in the right place, doing what I was divinely called to do. However, my involvement with the Graham and Campolo organizations introduced me to white folks with the same call, yet who were not suffering financially the way I was. I began to question: Why was this? Was God really in my ministry? The more I was exposed to white urban missions, the more unqualified I felt. The underlying message was that if God were in it, abundant resources would be there. A sign of God's presence was financial success, so I often felt defeated.

My promise to God and Promise Keepers

Because urban missions was God's call on my life, I continued, and over time, I met evangelicals who were interested in my work. They would invite me to coffee and ask who I was and what I was doing.

A few weeks later, some would contribute financially to our work. I enjoyed these new relationships. I felt blessed by their gifts and enjoyed speaking to groups about our life, work, and commitment to Jesus.

However, I noticed the organizations were monocultural, lacking diversity. I was the only person of color in the room on many occasions. My work was among very vulnerable black people, but my funding came from financially secure white people. The more I was exposed to "higher" levels in the Christian missions world, the whiter it was. Eventually it was all white. Along the way, I would always meet incredible people of color who were doing great work, but they were never the final decision makers. The final decisions were almost always made by white men, and occasionally by white women. I detected a trend of incredible program people—black, Latino, Asian—doing crazy good work, who answered to whites. It was a deep problem. People of color knew it and whites sensed it, but rarely did anyone address it.

I was only a few years into my work when Promise Keepers came on the scene. Suddenly race and reconciliation were in the public eye. Promise Keepers brought to light the race problem in the church and the need to do something about it. I was all in! I traveled with a group of leaders from my all-black Philadelphia church to Atlanta's Georgia Dome to attend a Promise Keepers convention. More white men than one can imagine embraced me. Atlanta was a key marker in my race-and-the-church journey. This was the first time I heard Christian whites openly confront other white folks about racism. Promise Keepers challenged Christians as I had never before heard. They created space for conversation and answered questions that could only be addressed by my Anglo brothers and sisters. These events gave me breathing space in processing racism in the *Missio Dei*.

I watched white man after white man go onstage and apologize in tears for his bigotry. White man after white man told story after story of his racism. The moments were mind-blowing and deeply moving. The confessions were I-told-you-so moments for me. I thought, "I knew it! I knew it!" The confessions satisfied something inside me and confirmed times when I knew I was being treated differently. They validated my feelings when I had sensed racism, but could not prove it—the times I knew a white dude was looking down on me, when I could feel it in my bones, but could do nothing about it. Standing in that stadium and listening to all those confessions gave me courage to process openly and honestly what I had been thinking and feeling since the first day I stepped off a bus to attend Archbishop John Carroll High School in Radnor, Pennsylvania. Standing in the Georgia Dome many years after that first day at my high school in 1978, I began to process my experiences with race and culture.

A "main line" education

Archbishop John Carroll High School is in Radnor, Pennsylvania, an upper-middle-class suburb twenty-five miles from Philadelphia "on the main line" between Villanova and St. Davids. Both boys and girls attended but in different sections of the building.

On my first day of school, I traveled from my West Philly home on the number 52 bus to City Line Avenue. The bus was full of

Segregated Church Services in the North

Free blacks in the North still faced prejudice and seg-regation in both the secular and sacred worlds. In northern churches black members were relegated to slave galleries, balconies, or "Negro pews."

The African American Episcopal Church is the oldest African American denomination. Established in Philadelphia in 1816, it was born out of a protest against black members being required to sit in a seg-regated gallery in the church.

Frederick Douglass, the formerly enslaved aboli-tionist and African American leader, recalled visiting a Methodist church in the North where the minister served Communion first to whites, then to blacks, while

black high school students, including friends dating back to grade school. From City Line Avenue I transferred to a bus that passed by Bala Cynwyd, Narberth, Ardmore, Haverford, Bryn Mawr, and Villanova—all beautiful, well-kept neighborhoods with manicured lawns and homes much larger than those where I lived. Finally we arrived in Radnor. In front, the grass was green and lush. The bus drove around the beautiful campus. The grounds seemed to stretch forever. There were fields for football, soccer, and field hockey and a baseball diamond. I never imagined a school could have that much land around it. Further, I had no idea on my first day of school that this place would forever change my worldview.

reminding them that God was no respecter of color. Douglass never returned there to witness the sacrament. In his narrative, he spoke harshly about Christianity as practiced by slaveholders: "I love the pure, peaceable, and impartial Christianity of Christ: I therefore hate the corrupt, slaveholding, women-whipping, cradle-plundering, partial and hypocritical Christianity of this land. Indeed, I can see no reason, but the most deceitful one, for calling the religion of this land Christianity. I look upon it as the climax of all misnomers, the boldest of all frauds, and the grossest of all libels..." Source: http://www.pbs.org/thisfarbyfaith/people/frederick _douglass.html

Douglass challenged whether what he saw was even Christianity at all.

The bus stopped at the back of the building and the driver opened the door. One by one the busload of black students stepped off the bus and into what appeared to be an endless crowd of awestruck white students. It was the most uncomfortable feeling I'd ever experienced. I felt like a specimen under a microscope. A sea of pale faces examined me as I searched for a place to hide. Neither the blacks nor the whites acknowledged each other as we darker-hued students pushed through the horde of whites to find an empty space. We hurried toward a spot near the Dumpsters.

I felt as though I had been dropped into a new dimension.

Of course, I'd seen white folks before, but never this close. They brushed against me as I made my way through the crowd. We were so close I could look into their eyes—some blue—hear the difference in their voices, notice the rather odd color of their hair. It wasn't like seeing a white person on television or standing behind a counter. Everyone was so close. Some of them looked downright sloppy with their shirts hanging outside of their pants and their ties dangling around their necks, knots halfway down their chests. Most of them wore run-down Dockers on their feet. Fear gripped me, as it seemed like all the whites continued to stare at us. There was nothing familiar and no place of solace to run to. I felt insecure and was full of questions.

What in the world had my parents done to me? Why were there so many of them and so few of us? Why did so many have blue eyes? Why did so many wear corduroy pants? Why was our bus the last to arrive? Did they really want me here? Did I really want to be here?

The white kids all acted like they knew each other. None of them seemed the least bit fearful, like I was. Some of the boys began tossing a Frisbee. I saw some guys smoking and wondered why no teachers stopped them.

The white students began moving inside, and they started mooing. Did white people like to act like cows, I mused, as I wondered how they knew where to go. As the day progressed, every time the kids changed classes, the mooing would start again. I realized then we were very much like cattle being herded from pasture to pasture and this was their way of poking fun.

The teachers divided all the students—black and white— alphabetically. The few people I knew from our bus had last names near the end of the alphabet. I was sent to a room with twenty white guys and me. Was it on purpose? Was this a plan to separate us so we'd have no backup in case of a fight?

This was homeroom.

My homeroom teacher was Brother Joe, a slender white man with short black hair. He seemed awfully young to be a Brother. He wore all black and a priest's collar. Even his shoes and socks were black, and he carried a black sweater. Brother Joe must have recognized the absolute fear in my eyes because he immediately came toward me with a big grin. "Welcome. Don't worry. I'm going to let you know everything you need to get along here." He guided me to my seat. His words and demeanor were friendly and exactly what I needed at the moment.

Over the next four years, Brother Joe would become one of my favorite people. Addressing the class, he explained where the lunchroom was, our class schedules, and how to find our way inside the building. He gave us a short history of the school. Closing his notebook, he said, "I have one last thing to say before you head out to your classes. I want each of you to look at each person in this class directly in the eye."

Great. This had to be some weird white person thing.

Brother Joe continued, "These men around you will be with you for the next four years. Your homeroom will not change. You should get to know one another, appreciate one another, and eventually love and support each other. You will see a lot of each other. You will play together, cry together, hurt together, and grow up together. Make every day count."

The bell rang and almost everyone headed out. Stunned, I remained in my seat. What did he mean? He expected me to do all those things with a bunch of white guys? Was he out of his mind? Though he appeared to be nice enough, he had to be crazy to think that would ever happen.

That scene ran through my mind as I stood in the Georgia Dome almost fifteen years later—now a dad, now a missionary, now with many friendships across races and cultures, and now with a need to be healed of that pain. I wept listening to their stories.

First leadership in missions

For a couple of years after my wife and I founded Restoration Ministries, our nonprofit, to answer that early call to missions, I became a program director at Mission Year, a nonprofit that gives young Christian adults the opportunity to volunteer in an under-resourced urban neighborhood in the United States. I enjoyed the respect and strong support of both staff and leadership.

When the executive director resigned, I applied for the job based on my experience as an urban leader, which equaled that of the outgoing executive director. I was rejected. A Christian leader, who was a good friend of mine, said, "I would never hire you to do that job. I don't feel a black person could ever do that job." His feeling was perhaps based on a belief that hiring a black executive director might affect funding. Many caring friends, both black and white, counseled me to leave, cautioning me that I had hit the stained glass ceiling, never to advance further in that missions organization. After much consideration and contemplation, I decided to stay because the values of the organization were deeply rooted in loving people. I didn't feel I could leave the relationships

I had formed there with staff, churches, and service agencies. My life was so entwined in them. They were more important than my personal hurt and embarrassment.

As it happened, the newly hired executive director, who had fewer years in missions work and less urban ministry experience than I, brought excellent skills in finance and fund-raising (that I was able to learn) and quickly moved on. I was unexpectedly asked to serve as interim director and was told that I had a year to show that I had vision, to revitalize the fractured staff, to establish administrative support (an area where I was weak), and to create new funding streams.

I began to revision and reimagine Mission Year. The core values remained the same, but how we operated culturally changed. We stayed in communities longer in order to build deeper relationships. Instead of separate orientations and closings in each city, we brought everyone together semiannually. Most important, instead of youthful volunteers deciding where and how they wanted to serve, the Mission Year leadership, in conjunction with community organizations in the areas to be served, determined where and how the volunteers would serve. Mission Year received grants from the community for this work. This changed our funding structure and reduced our dependence on personal support, which allowed more people of color to serve as volunteers.

After proving myself, the board hired me as executive director. Finally, I had the leadership position I had for so long felt called to, in the organization I cared about. The board gave me full support as a leader, and I felt affirmed by them.

Unfortunately, the board could not control external reactions to a black man moving into this position of leadership. Immediately, promised funding was pulled. Some funders and longtime partners retreated. While not all departed, the impact was significant. Instead of "Congratulations on being appointed president," I was constantly asked, "Is the organization going to stay in business? Are you going to be around?" Everyone was kind and supportive on the surface, but instead of backing me, they politely awaited my failure, anticipated it even. I would attend meetings or make calls only to realize that a crucial conversation had already taken place. This was very painful for me personally and counterproductive to the organization.

Those who backed away or worked unconstructively behind the scenes were mostly white men, some of whom I had considered close friends. They were noticeably quiet, although one confessed to me I was "just a token." I no longer felt edified and supported by them. Instead, I felt I needed to prove myself day after day.

A few years after I had been in the position, the charismatic, brilliant Christian leader who had said he'd never hire me or any black person for an executive director position apologized: "I think you are doing a great job."

I have had many experiences where people in positions of power used that power effectively, and I've learned from them. I've always been a leader; sometimes a good one, at other times a poor one. I often have dreamed of being in a position where I use my gift of leadership to influence others rooted in my faith. The leader in me often envisioned ways to do missions work differently, ways of improving that work to make it culturally relevant for all people. The leadership role came naturally to me, whether I was on a job where the boss wasn't connecting well with subordinates or in a ministry where the leadership didn't connect with the population being served.

But nothing is more difficult, more frustrating, than being put in a position of leadership without actually being given the power to lead. This is the situation in which many people of color find themselves when they lead predominantly white organizations or entities that historically have been led by whites. The inability of whites—with a few notable exceptions—to recognize, support, partner, and cooperate with leaders of color has wounded missions deeply.

I share my personal story not to create separation, but rather to uncover the issues and open up space for dialogue. Just as Promise Keepers sought the first needle in the haystack of racial reconciliation, we in missions need to examine this issue to create space for healing in order to move closer to beloved community and the *Missio Dei*.

Not as qualified

Some believe the lack of diverse leadership in missions is a skill-based issue. They argue that people of color lack management skills or administrative experience.

As a visionary, there are certain gifts I do not have and skills I have never developed. This is often perceived as my biggest hindrance as a leader. So many white men I know lack the same skills, but for them it is not seen as a deficiency. Management consultant and author Peter Drucker's words on leadership, "Lead with your strengths and manage your weaknesses," were a lifeline to me. It gave language to what I was feeling. No leader has all the gifts and skills necessary to lead, but culture tends to value some skills over others.

I grew up in Southwest Philly where there were no rich friends to ask for money. I had no experience opening fund-raising doors. I quickly learned that deficiency meant I had no influence in the eyes of the white not-for-profit boards. I'm good at urban ministry, so that was a strength I leaned on. At heart I'm a pastor, so I know how to listen to people and care for them. I built on those skills by developing and implementing a strong program to care and relate to people. In doing so, I have found the people I connected with across race, class, and gender lines to be incredibly life-giving—because we share common vision and heart to serve. The donors with whom I had personal opportunities to share began to see my heart. Support came from staff who appreciated my leadership style. Hope and a renewed belief came from partners and friends. I found my own leadership style and voice. I discovered that people share their resources through relationships. My natural bent toward establishing relationships that invite people in eventually helped support my work. This was a new strength I developed.

What is often misunderstood by white-controlled nonprofit and missions organizations is that leaders of color often lead differently. I build relational power. I have learned that people make decisions around relationships and trust. They no longer buy into the paradigm that their role is to listen and execute what any given top-level person says.

Traditional white male leaders often rely on established funding and other power structures and are skilled in navigating them. This style says, "Don't encourage subordinates to build their own power bases because it undermines influence from the top." It shifts dynamics. Leaders who are still connected to the old way of doing things want to influence everyone at every point. Relational power subverts that type of leadership.

Authentic relational power overturns power from the top to create power *together*. I learned to run the organization based on strong relationships. I cared for my staff and loved them well. I did my best to be authentic. I didn't micromanage them, but rather I trusted their gifts, encouraged them, and acknowledged their hard work. I learned from many mistakes.

Leaders of color may not be as experienced in navigating the old power structures, managing according to paradigms of the past, and administering archaic systems. We are not white people in red, yellow, black, or brown skin. We bring a new approach to leadership, shaped by our cultures. Christian missions need the new skills, gifts, and calling that diversity brings. It is a grave miscalculation to disqualify leaders of color based on gaps in their talents. They are better viewed as newly and freshly qualified in ways that will add new life to our *Missio Dei*.

> "A white leader can be successful with good working knowledge and a decent network, but a leader of color has to be exceptional to have the same amount of success. We can change this. We must change this."
>
> —*an African American missions leader*

People of color historically have led differently than their white counterparts. We usually reshape and distribute leadership. It's a cultural difference shared by many leaders who are not white males, by women and by different races and cultures. I could share anecdote after anecdote about this shift.

I feel the push back as I write these words. I hear it all the time. It goes like this: "I know black pastors that lead out of power, who are domineering and insist on calling all the shots." Such leaders have learned to mimic an autocratic style from cultural norms. Their influence is limited and they are, in fact, always described as "black leaders," which limits their influence on society and culture in general. (A white leader is usually not called a "white leader" and therefore is perceived as able to lead anyone and influence society and culture on a broader scale.) Leaders of color usually distribute power well, however, because they understand and believe in shared leadership. Most have also experienced the pain of being excluded from the decision-making process.

People who hold positions of power often feel pressure to present an illusion that they know more than those served and have all the answers. This is false.

I do not want to be the person who pretends to be God—to know everything. I certainly do not want to be led by a person who claims to know everything. I don't know much about accounting, but I am learning to steward funds raised. I don't know much about marketing, but I am learning. I am learning at all times. I will never master everything. I have learned from my mistakes and continue to do so. I don't portray myself as a know-it-all leader but rather as part of a team whose role is to be a visionary and step out ahead.

Power is its own principality, which is always with us. It can claim you. But relationships transform power into collective empowerment, enabling us to realize the power of God in our midst.

After seven years, the organization I was blessed to lead, and learn by doing so, was strong in different ways. The entire staff was comprised 30 to 40 percent of people of color. Authentic power existed throughout. Our focus was on how we served one another and our neighbors. The bond was deep. The organization was relationally driven, more than institutionally driven. My wife and family were as much a part of Mission Year as I was, and I had a personal relationship with each person on staff. That led me to consider each one's personal development and growth. As a leader, I saw their family, professional career, and spiritual life as part of my responsibility.

The depths we were able to reach at Mission Year reflect what missions need to be—looking at people first. Black pastors and leaders I knew as a child and in my youth did that for me. Pastors like the late Hiawatha Coleman could look into who a person was. That is a gift of black pastors not talked about and valued in the missions world. Not looking at what a person can bring to you, but rather at who they are is cultural.

Five years after I was hired as executive director at Mission Year, Word Made Flesh, a community of Christians called to serve among the most vulnerable of the world's urban poor, asked me to serve on their board. I found myself in conversation with the board several years later about becoming their next executive director. I wasn't looking to leave Mission Year; I wasn't looking for a job. The director of Word Made Flesh had left a year earlier, and at the end of the search process, the right candidate had not emerged.

I brought my beliefs about *Missio Dei* in operation within the power structures of Christian organizations to the Word Made Flesh hiring process. I did not want to be awarded the position based on my relationship with the board, as so often happens in such establishments. I wanted to be certain I was the most qualified. "I don't want to be given this position," I informed them. "I want this hire to be a community decision—staff, leaders, and others need to have input and ask questions." Although I was a board member, I submitted my résumé, bio, and references and interviewed with the board. That proved effective because board members don't delve into leadership issues with each other as they do with a potential hire. They asked me all the hard questions they'd ask any potential candidate. They learned my core beliefs. Then I interviewed with their regional coordinators from Asia, Africa, Europe, and South America, fielding questions from staff around the world. When I received the offer, I felt honored by the community because it was a decision from everybody that I should be their leader.

When I compare my two hiring experiences, I felt the Word Made Flesh community valued my being a leader of color. My experience and perspective as a black man was something the community desired. Who I am culturally was received as a gift to the organization. Seven years prior, I was filling a spot that needed to be filled. My cultural background—an African American from a struggling urban community—played negatively into the process and was perceived as something to be overcome. Granted, seven years later, I definitely had a stronger voice and a stronger vision, but who I am as a black man was a positive part of the process. Word Made Flesh looked into the person I am, and I was reminded of the way black pastors and leaders had looked into me early in my life, the way I had for my staff at Mission Year.

As I move into the next chapter of missions, I draw from twenty-five years of experience. I look into the people who have served as leaders. In fulfilling the *Missio Dei*, I am committed to mutual exchange between indigenous leaders and missions organizations, led by the broadly diverse spectrum of Christians God is sending.

CHAPTER 3

Diversity at Work in the *Missio Dei*

"Only where whites were in relationships with people of color have I seen a white person motivated to give up their power. A friendship is built, and the motivation becomes 'I love and care about this person. I am willingly giving up some of my power. I am encouraging them and affirming them and building them up.' Unfortunately, you can't regulate friendship."

—*Donna Barber*

I n my journey I have met many special people who live the *Missio Dei*. They appeal to others, regardless of race or culture, going beyond themselves to inspire us all. Those are the saints among us—ones who transcend the problems that create great pain in the world. They are able to move past race and respond to the Spirit moving in their lives. Their acts of grace and love move us closer to God. While power in our society has rested with whites and hurt and pain have been crafted by many of them, I've also experienced comfort, friendship, and grace from many of my white brothers and sisters.

Several years ago I served on the board of Discovering Opportunities for Outreach and Reflection (DOOR), an urban ministry I had never heard of until a friend asked me to help them get started in Atlanta. Their tagline "see the face of God in the city" intrigued me, so I agreed. That summer I made a presentation in Denver to a board of mostly white men, asking them to expand work to Atlanta. They approved our application to start DOOR there. We had another request: that our local board and staff be diverse. The board appeared intrigued by our appeal, and I sensed they had heard talk of diversity before and valued the idea. But a real commitment to it seemed like a dream when they agreed the suggestion was worth engaging.

Our local board started with the appointment of women and men, blacks, whites, and Latinos. After a couple years, Glenn Balzer, the white national executive director, began asking questions about diversifying the entire organization—from the national board, year-round staff, and local boards down to summer interns. The national board had a number of hard, honest conversations, which was the start of something special within the organization.

The story of DOOR

DOOR encourages, actually insists, that local people take leadership roles. Young people who volunteer in urban programs sponsored by DOOR are primarily privileged whites. But the leadership, the summer support staff, and those who supervise the white volunteers are members of the community. They are black, Latino, and Asian. It's a reversal of how many missions organizations function. And it's a model that works.

When DOOR began as a national organization in 1986, it was the typical missions program: the board and staff were comprised primarily of white men. In 2004, the board, desiring diversity but not knowing how to meet that challenge, created an Urban Leadership Development Task Force comprised of their board members of color. The task force examined all aspects of the organization and listed some pretty big issues to tackle. Diversification didn't happen overnight, nor did the process embarrass or demonize the organization. The organization continued to thrive in the midst of change. Remarkably, the board and staff were committed to having hard conversations and to absorbing the inevitable backlash to such a shift.

Glenn recalls the conversations around diversity.

In my naïveté at that time, I thought, well, "How do we change the makeup of the participants of DOOR?" We brought that question to our Urban Leadership Task Force. At that first meeting, that group essentially stopped me in my tracks and asked, "Are you serious about diversity?" They said, "We don't care what color your participants are or what their ethnic background is. Until you change how decision-making happens, you functionally change nothing."

The task force and staff took the board into deeper discussions of who DOOR was as an organization and how decisions were made. Glenn reflects:

The goal was that in ten years—basically by 2014—51 percent of our board members would be people of color from the communities we serve. By the ninth year, I don't think we had a single board chair that was a white male. All were either women or persons of color.

Looking at DOOR's decision-making process locally and nationally has been huge. There's been significant change. When I started at DOOR [in 1986], the people I reported to looked like me. I'm a tall, white male. Today the people I am accountable to—the people who set my salary, my benefits, who do my annual reviews—don't look anything like me. And that's pretty substantial.

Glenn discovered that once the decision-making process was changed, hiring practices also changed. At DOOR, local pastors and ministry leaders are empowered to make decisions at local board levels.

In 1994, the summer staff was 100 percent college students from places like Southern Methodist University. They basically were Anglos who wanted to come and do good works during the summer. In 2013, 74 percent of our summer staff were young adults from the community. They were young adults of color. This created all sorts of dynamics when we put young adults of color in leadership positions over groups that were primarily Anglo.

Unlike many missions organizations, funding for DOOR is not dependent on donors—traditionally white, middle-aged or older, and conservative. That eliminates a lot of stress on nonwhite staff.

They are not responsible for funding their own salaries. Summer program participants—mostly church youth groups—pay $305 per person to attend. About three thousand young people participate each year. This equates to about 70 percent of the organization's funding. The yearlong program raises about 15 percent of the funds. The other 15 percent comes from grants or individual donors. Staff is paid, programs are supported, and more people of color can become summer program leaders.

Glenn continues:

Those who come to the summer program come from forty-eight states and represent more than twenty denominations. We accept both faith-based and non-faith-based participants. They are 85 percent Anglo. They are people of privilege who need to come to the city to see what is happening in the city. The summer program support staff—those who lead these groups that come to the city—are primarily young adults who come from the city. Our summer staff are leading them around the city and helping them process their experience.

For affluent white students, many who have never lived in urban environments, participating in DOOR in the inner-city sections of San Antonio, Chicago, Denver, Atlanta, Miami, or Hollywood, California, is an eye-opening experience. Add to this being supervised by a person of color from that community. Unforgettable experiences abound—some good, some bad. Glenn says:

The reaction ranges from white students who say "Oh my! This is amazing!" to "Why am I doing this anyway? Is this causing more harm than it is doing good?" Eighty percent of our evaluations are really good. Participants say, "Thank you. Our group got to experience things from a whole other perspective." The other 20 percent I would describe as being in the "How dare you!" category.

Glenn shares an incident when a group came to the west side of Chicago to DOOR in the heart of the city. They arrived Sunday evening. By Monday morning half of them had left, gone home. Their group leader called him and demanded to know why he would put the group in such a dangerous neighborhood. Glenn remembers:

> Our Chicago city director was an African American woman. The groups would hardly recognize her as a leader. They would never say it, but their actions spoke real clearly: "How dare you put someone like this in charge of us? She doesn't know the dangers that our kids are going to be facing!" So we've experienced some of that kind of obvious antagonism. But the vast majority says, "Thank you for exposing our kids to something so vastly different and yet so meaningful."

DOOR has an annual gathering called the Beloved Community Council, which is modeled after the Urban Leadership Development Task Force. It is a fellowship of all the board members and staff of color. They gather every year and talk about what it means to be a person of color in charge of a summer program wherein the majority of participants are Anglos. They ask each other how to lead successfully in that situation. It's proven to be a powerful conversation, one Glenn wishes they could have more often.

DOOR's model is unique and effective in missions, but rarely do those in mission fields ask Glenn about it—how it works, how they can incorporate some of its tenets. He concludes:

> I wish people would ask me. When people hear about what DOOR has become, there's a weird kind of silence. My Anglo friends don't know what to say. Then there's every kind of reaction. Some people think I'm a hero. Others ask, "How can you do that?" My friends of color say, "About time." It's interesting watching those dynamics.
>
> Personally, I'm at a place that the idea of having women in charge or people of color in charge shouldn't be seen as special, just formative.
>
> When I first started at DOOR I met a local Denver west side organizer; her name was Patricia Running Bear. Her exact words to me were, "So you are the new DOOR director. Don't tell us how to do anything until you have been here ten years." She then turned around and walked away. That advice has stayed with me.
>
> When I meet with folks who want to come to the city because God has called them to urban ministry, I usually start by telling them to hang out and just be for a few years. To date, this has never gone over well. Most white people who feel a call to urban ministry have a secret desire to become an urban hero. This desire is never voiced; rather, it is cleverly disguised in "call language."
>
> The weirdest silence comes when I start talking about power and equality—not in theological terms, but practical ones. For the most part, Anglos are powerful and they want to use their power benevolently. But they are not ready to empty themselves of their power. Creating spaces where all have equal say and

power always means that the powerful (read Anglo) have to give up power.

Today DOOR is working. But it works because we are being very, very, very intentional about it. Some people add color to their organizations, but they're not adding diversity in the sense that everyone is empowered. It means you have to create spaces for those conversations where you can ask, "Am I making you a token?" or "Is the power you have just symbolic or real?" Those conversations are difficult; they're painful.

I have to spend an awful lot of time reevaluating who I am, and that's nothing like I had imagined leadership to be. Somehow, I felt leadership meant I was in charge and everybody would listen to me. And that's not really what it is. Authentic change means looking at yourself in the mirror and that's not always fun.

I have so much white privilege that I don't always recognize when I'm using it. It's embarrassing when I get caught using it— less now than [when I began], but it's still there. There are still moments when I respond to things like an ignorant sexist. I've been around twenty years, but I still get caught in that. Those old privileges, they never fully go away. I understand the struggle of Paul in Romans 7, where he says, "That which I want to do, I don't do. That which I don't want to do, I do."

I believe someday I'm going to emerge. I haven't yet, but I'm hopeful. Change and growth have to start with me before I expect it to happen with anybody else.

CHAPTER 4

Redefining Urban Missions

"I have told you these things, so that in me you may have peace. In this world you will have trouble. But take heart! I have overcome the world."

—*John 16:33, NIV*

Missions, as defined by white evangelical and mainline denominations, is centered around service to another person or group. Urban missions often involve Christians going to an area in a city where there is a perceived need and helping meet that need. Missions also include soup kitchens, clothes closets, and food giveaways on special days like Christmas and Thanksgiving. They also may include prison ministry, homeless shelter support, or visits to senior centers.

Missions in the context of many churches of color can have the same definition, but missions are defined differently based on race and culture. Many black, Hispanic, Asian, and Native American churches, especially those located in urban centers, see their local work as their main mission. As one African American pastor stated, "I just walk out my door and the mission field is right there."

Missions, as defined by white evangelicals, is problematic. As defined in the first chapter, *Missio Dei* ("mission of God" or "the sending of God") is part of God's very nature. The missionary initiative is God's, not ours. Christians who come into a community to do missions work and Christians engaged in local work are both manifesting God's *Missio Dei*. Rather than viewing themselves as serving another group, white evangelists in urban missions ought to view themselves as servants of God, laboring with those whom God has planted in urban communities.

The characterization of missions by white evangelicals is at the root of urban missions challenges, especially around funding. Many missions organizations require missionaries to raise all their own living expenses to carry out their ministry. This involves getting family and friends to give donations and assumes that those called to urban missions have networks familiar with this idea of "raising support" and are able to give at a level that will adequately support the one serving.

Rather than fund Christians already living and working in the community to be served, white evangelicals favor funding urban missions like field trips for those outside the community. Money is given to support the field trippers rather than those who serve long term in such urban missions.

The Missions middleman

Urban missionaries who must raise money usually do so by sharing stories with funders about people whom they have contacted or helped. The better the storyteller, the better chance of being funded. I have always felt that white missionaries telling the stories of those served simply to get funding is dishonest. Not that they are dishonest people, but their methodology lacks integrity. Usually the pictures and videos of white missionaries objectify "poor people of color." This is disrespectful. True *Missio Dei* respects those served and empowers individuals to find their own voices, to tell their own stories.

Not only is this an unjust model for funding urban missions, it impedes the ability of Christians who serve in their own communities to raise money to fund their work. They are telling their own stories and those of their communities, yet they are not being funded. More often, white donors prefer to fund a white solicitor coming from the outside to "help" and "serve" rather than a local who is more familiar with the community and the culture.

The work of indigenous missionaries is further hampered by traditional missions agencies, which have become great middlemen. They have set themselves up between those who give and those who receive funding. The agencies and the outside missions workers connected with them are bigger winners than the communities served. The missionaries usually spend many, many years in an urban community, but never make it their home. In the end, they develop minimal indigenous leadership and little sustainability. Instead, they foster generations of care recipients.

Long-term family implications

Years ago, I met Sheila, who was incredibly happy that she was able to qualify for an interest-free mortgage through an urban Christian missions program. A single mom who had challenges, she worked every day and did her best to support her family. Sheila became a homeowner, raised her children in a decent place, and created a wonderful home for them.

Fifteen years later I ran into Sheila's daughter, Angel. As we greeted one another, Angel happily reported that she was going to move into a home through the same ministry.

Here we were a generation later, and Sheila's daughter was receiving the same service her mom received. I walked away saddened as I reflected on how celebrated that ministry had been. I could not shake my disappointment that nothing had changed for the family. They now had two generations of recipients. I don't see a good story here. The ministry has now told (sold) two stories of success to their donors. But I see only failure. A repeat recipient of charity, a generational expectation of assistance means the program has not been successful. Missions middlemen should not think only of their own existence. They must challenge themselves, or be challenged by funders, to look at long-term implications. Instead of telling other people's stories and defining success in terms of fund-raising, they must prayerfully ask hard questions.

Missionary invaders overlook neighborhood champions.

In today's urban landscape, some Christians move into struggling urban neighborhoods. Some have no intention of helping or becoming part of the community; they just find good deals on houses. However, some among them have great hearts and intend to do God's work in the neighborhood.

Almost all neighborhoods already have champions, people who have lived there a long time, or were born there and returned, and perhaps are second or third generation. They represent God and do good among their neighbors. They may not have much in terms of resources (often because of their sacrificial giving or concentration on service rather than generating income), yet they find ways to help, support, and empower people despite their own economic condition. Much of their work goes unnoticed or overlooked. Then, into this scenario comes urban missions—the white Christian cavalry who bring the Gospel through "morality" and resources.

They initially overlook most good people in the community and often view the neighborhood champions as old-timers set in their ways and protecting their turf. The urban missionaries cannot see much good about the neighborhood, other than the real estate values, and are appalled at the ethics and lives of the people around them. Their e-mails and letters to supporters immediately relay stories of unsafe places, horrible conditions, and dangerous, depraved people. They can't believe how those they have come to serve really live and treat one another. They highlight the crime, bad living conditions, trash, and drug activity. They use these horrific stories to raise money. Christian donors give to help these urban "saviors" and work starts to happen. The missionaries are scared, so they quickly secure their homes and organize neighborhood watches; they initiate spruce ups because people don't keep the area clean. They tell the stories of disadvantaged children, implying their parents—rather than corrupt systems—are the culprits.

And urban missionaries are praised for helping a horrible place recover.

Scriptures Read to the Enslaved in the United States

Ephesians 6:5, NIV: Slaves, obey your earthly masters with respect and fear, and with sincerity of heart, just as you would obey Christ.

Ephesians 6:9, NIV: And masters, treat your slaves in the same way. Do not threaten them, since you know that he who is both their Master and yours is in heaven, and there is no favoritism with him.

Colossians 3:22, NIV: Slaves, obey your earthly masters in everything; and do it, not only when their eye is on you and to curry their favor, but with sincerity of heart and reverence for the Lord.

Colossians 4:1, NIV: Masters, provide your slaves with what is right and fair, because you know that you also have a Master in heaven.

Titus 2:9, NIV: Teach slaves to be subject to their masters in everything, to try to please them, not to talk back to them.

1 Peter 2:18, NIV: Slaves, in reverent fear of God submit yourselves to your masters, not only to

Missionary invaders speak on behalf of the neighborhood.

Next is where the major offense takes place. Inevitably, over time as they gradually cleanse their cultural lenses, urban missionaries

48

those who are good and considerate, but also to those who are harsh.

Despite these cherry-picked verses, read completely out of historical social context and in opposition to the message of the Bible as a whole, those in bondage generally did not embrace these readings. Instead, they found and clung to the story of God's deliverance of the Hebrews and Jesus's teachings on justice and liberation. In secret, the enslaved developed indigenous expressions of Christian faith. They met at night in "hush harbors" deep in thickets and created Negro spirituals (songs of sorrow and coded messages of freedom). The enslaved held fast to a Gospel that promised earthly deliverance and a God who heard their prayers and cared.

No black preacher (unless he proved trustworthy) could openly preach to the enslaved unless a white person was present. Thanks be to God that some whites participated fully in the abolitionist movement to end the travesty of slavery. They put their lives on the line and helped free many from legal bondage. This multicultural, divinely led effort changed the world and began to show God moving in a unified effort, with a power beyond this world.

begin to see the beauty in the people of the community. They begin learning a few lessons—many the hard way and at great cost to their long-term neighbors. By the time they begin to correct their behavior and attitudes, they have reinforced stereotypes. They have also avoided counsel and disrespected or created animosities with neighborhood champions. And they have established a financial backing to remain. They have become urban missionary invaders.

These invaders begin to represent and speak on behalf of the poor in the neighborhood. They are asked to sit in places of power, serve on boards, to speak, and to write. They may now begin to admire neighborhood champions and even open themselves up to learn from them, but they don't yield the opportunity to sit in places of power to those neighborhood champions.

The end result is white Christians, people from the outside, speaking on behalf of people of color about their own communities. Often those who have not even done a great job connecting with the community they "serve" begin representing that community in publications and on boards.

This is not *Missio Dei*. This kind of urban invasion causes division between Christians called to urban missions from inside and from outside the served communities. It separates those serving from those served. Their missions efforts reek of paternalism. We must challenge and stop this practice. It hurts existing leaders in neighborhoods and stymies the work God has begun in them. Those entering a neighborhood to start a work should not be funded at the expense of those from the community already doing good work. Those who ignore leadership that already exists and assume superiority to local efforts can no longer be tolerated. The thinking must be: "God is already at work in that community. How do I join in what God is doing there?"

CHAPTER 5

A Self-Examination of Our "Service" to the "Served"

"My hope is that we are changing the paradigm. It's going to take a lot to do so."

—*Jenny Ouseph*

S erving is a biblical concept. Jesus said in Matthew 20:28, he came to serve, not to be served. In a missions context, the word *served* has come to mean, "You are doing something for another that puts you in a position of power." That understanding of service creates better-than/less-than roles. In contrast, Jesus served as a complement to the humanity of others. When he washed the disciples' feet, he was displaying leadership, not superiority. Our service in missions doesn't make us superior to those served, but rather puts us *in relationship* with them. It gives us an opportunity to relate to others as brothers and sisters—human to human, all created by God, all loved by God in all of our flaws.

Early Missions in Asia

Europeans bringing Christianity to Asia found a people with centuries-old traditions and self-confidence. Asians doubted if Europeans had anything of value

Those of us who serve in missions show God's love for those served just as they are, in all their flaws, right in the midst of their flawed circumstances. And as we serve, we are humbled by God's love for us, with all of our continued flaws, despite knowing God. We become deeply aware of the flaws in our culture, for missions that fulfill the true *Missio Dei* starkly illuminate that culture and Christian community are not the same.

To serve means to recognize the unjust, ungodly systems that have privileged men over women, those with white skin over those of color, those who have material wealth over those who do not, and humans over all of God's universal creation. God, not temporal privileges, shapes the identity of the missionary. These privileges are given up for the privilege of serving.

Below are common views of missions, especially as they relate to culture and race, followed by my thoughts on what is needed to bring a new perspective to conversations on urban missions. The rest of the book is organized by these points.

Missions funds go to settlers who tell stories of people they encounter.

Missions funds go to neighborhood champions.

Those served are led to become dependent on missionary services and programs.

to offer. Outside the borders of strong European rule, early Catholics were on their own to make inroads. It is a history of success and expulsion by strong indigenous powers that said "no thanks" to foreign religion and culture.

Those served are empowered to become self-reliant and God trusting.

Missions workers' assumptions about the served community are negative.

Missions workers highlight the positive in the served community.

Missionary culture is unexamined and presumed superior to the culture of those served.

Missions workers engage in self-examination that includes missionary culture and begins with the assumption that the culture of those served is equal to their own.

Missionary culture is imposed upon those served.

Cultural differences are celebrated.

Missionary service is motivated by guilt.

Missionaries serve because they recognize that the unjust systems that have produced their privilege while denying opportunities to those served are not God's will.

Missionaries serve because of obligation.

Missionaries serve in obedience to the call of God.

Missionaries serve because they pity those served.

Missionaries serve because they love and respect those served.

Missionaries serve when they are old/retired or young/students.

Missionaries are multigenerational.

Missionaries serve in foreign countries.

Missionaries serve both globally and locally.

Missionaries are white.

Missionaries are multiethnic.

Missions leaders are from outside the community served.

Missions leaders are from the community served.

PART II

A NEW PERSPECTIVE TO URBAN MISSIONS

CHAPTER 6

Diversifying Boards

"I've sat in a room when we've talked to a funder and there have been people of color at the table. You think you're building relationships. Then the people of color leave, and the discussion changes—the discussion fundamentally changes."

—Glenn Balzer

I n chapter 4, we glimpsed the process of raising support, by which missions funds go to missionary settlers who tell stories of people they encounter rather than to neighborhood champions through whom God is transforming people and their communities. The National Football League is a good but perhaps unlikely model of how this problem with urban missions funding can be fixed.

A number of years ago, the NFL recognized it was a problem that 67 percent of their players were African American, but only 6 percent of their head coaches were. Rather than take years studying why this was happening or commit dollars ad nauseam to figuring out how could they change it, in great get-that-first-down fashion, they instituted the Rooney Rule to ensure that minorities, especially African Americans, were considered for high-level coaching positions.

The rule is named for Dan Rooney, the owner of the Pittsburgh Steelers and the chairman of the league's diversity committee, and also for the Rooney family, which has a long history of providing African Americans with opportunities to serve in team leadership roles with the Steelers.

Until 1979, Fritz Pollard was the only minority head coach in NFL history, and he had served more than fifty years before in the 1920s. When the Rooney Rule was implemented in 2003, only Tom Flores, Art Shell, Dennis Green, Ray Rhodes, Tony Dungy, and Herman Edwards had ever held head top coaching jobs. (Only Dungy and Edwards were actively head coaching at the time of the rule's implementation, though Shell and Green would later return to head coaching.) Dungy had struggled for years before getting a head coaching job. Chuck Noll had recommended Dungy many times as a head coach candidate while he was Noll's assistant in the 1980s with the Steelers. But Dungy would not become a head coach until 1996, when he took over the Tampa Bay Buccaneers.

At the start of the 2006 season, the overall percentage of African American coaches had jumped to 22 percent. Since the Rooney Rule, several NFL franchises have hired African American head coaches, including the Steelers, who hired Mike Tomlin before their 2007 season. (The Steelers had already interviewed Ron Rivera, who is Hispanic, and Rooney shared that Tomlin's hiring did not result from the rule.)

It's ironic that Christian missions need to learn from the NFL instead of leading the way in standards of equity. According to a study by TechMission, there are 1.4 million nonprofits in the United States. Approximately 1.1 million are led by whites, 138,000 are led by blacks, 50,000 are Latino led, and 12,000 are led by other groups. While nonwhites comprise 53 percent of U.S. poverty levels—the issue most of these nonprofits address—groups led by blacks and others of color receive only about 3 percent of the funding. The funding provided to Christian organizations led by people of color follows this statistical pattern. Urban missions need a Rooney Rule. Christian funders need a systematic look at diversity in missions leadership.

Can Christians self-correct?

The pattern in the United States is that diversity is begun when the government imposes sanctions or passes laws. Can we Christians correct ourselves? Can we, as followers of Jesus and based on God's word, with the leading of the Spirit, make sure there is equality in urban missions funding? What impact would such a change have?

To start, at least 25 percent of all funding would immediately go to urban missions organizations led by people of color. Funders need to seek out neighborhood champions in the communities they serve, build relationships with leaders of color, and insist that the organizations they fund that work with populations of color have leaders of color in senior positions.

Furthermore, training institutions must make grants available for leaders of color to learn fund-raising—major donor expansion, capital campaigns, annual funding, board development, and planned giving.

Boards must open their social networks to newcomers.

Providing others access to these networks goes a long way to breaking the cycles of ministry poverty, where so many organizations led by people of color find themselves.

Nicole was recruited and offered a job to lead a newly established urban ministry. She accepted and immediately began working on a vision/mission statement, hiring and training staff, funding sources and generating PR. She succeeded in all of the above, although funding was slow. However, she was never given a seat on the board. (The executive director should always have a nonvoting seat on the board.)

As Nicole got more and more recognition for her accomplishments, white staffers and funders began to question her dedication and commitment. This eventually led to major disruption. Nicole left, and after she did, white staffers and funders commented that Nicole had been hired to work there, but not lead. The board hired Nicole, but they were the leaders, along with the large funders. They called the shots. They were to be the public face of the ministry.

As Nicole rose to leadership via her work, with a resultant higher personal profile, her support from whites began to diminish.

Nonprofit boards are 86 percent white.

The white staff who served under Nicole's leadership had access to, relationships, and social engagements with Nicole's bosses (the board members and funders) that Nicole didn't have. Conversations, uninformed opinions, and one-sided perspectives were shared within these relationships and social settings and began to shape the way Nicole was perceived by board members and funders. Nicole never had a chance relationally in these whites-only exchanges that seemed perfectly normal to them. Substantially diversified boards will at the very least give the Nicoles of the world a chance to be heard.

Missio Dei means multiethnic.

Young, Asian American, and outspoken, Pam participated in urban missions from 2003 to 2004, serving as a team leader in an African American community in Philadelphia. "Out of thirty team members, only three of us were not white," she says. "It was a difficult year because the organization tries to teach social justice and most volunteers came with no basic knowledge that the lack of economic or social justice created the environment in which people were living." There was a lot of resistance to seeing that race was actually an issue. The city director (her supervisor) was white. "We are very good friends now, but I didn't expect the learning curve to be so steep. I thought everyone would be on the same page. I felt like the staff and the city director did not know how to support me. "

She spoke out about how it feels to be a person of color in a predominantly white team environment and tried to get the organization to make needed changes in the curriculum. Ironically, it may have been her willingness to speak out that got her noticed by the organization's leadership. She was invited to speak at the Urbana Missions Conference, a well-known gathering of college students seeking involvement in missions. "Sometimes the staff didn't have a person of color, so they asked me to go. They wanted to shine me; they wanted me to be part of the work."

China

Christianity came to China around 635 AD, when a Nestorian monk named Aluoben (believed to have come from Persia) entered the ancient capital of Changan—now modern-day Xi'an—in central China. His works were an inscription of roughly 1,800 Chinese characters on a large stone tablet, called a stela, unearthed in the 1600s AD by a Christian monk. In 845, an imperial edict limited all foreign religion, including Christianity. By 907, Christianity had all but disappeared from China. Source: http://www.pbs.org/frontlineworld/stories/china_705/history/china.html

Christianity reappeared in the thirteenth century, when the Mongols conquered China and established the Yuan dynasty (1279–1368). The Mongols were open to Christian missionaries and even turned over the administration of parts of northern China to Christian tribesmen from central Asia. The pope sent Franciscan missionaries in an effort to form an alliance with the Mongol empire. Italian merchants also founded some Catholic communities. When the armies of the

She was elected to the alumni board in 2004 and later was asked to be on the organization's board. She seemed like a great person to sit on the board of a Christian urban organization. She looked forward to the responsibility, an opportunity to bring change—and yes, questions of race and culture—to the forefront.

Ming dynasty (1368–1644) expelled the Mongols, China's second period of Christian growth came to an end.

A new wave of Jesuit missionaries came to China toward the end of the Ming dynasty. The first great missionary, Italian Jesuit Matteo Ricci, and other Jesuits respected the Chinese culture. They dressed as Confucian scholars, complete with long beards and showing reverence for scholarship. Ricci learned to speak and write Chinese and gained the respect of the Chinese upper class. He became the first Westerner invited into the Forbidden City. At its peak near the end of the seventeenth century, Chinese missions were serving perhaps a quarter of a million people— quite a number, yet still a tiny proportion of the population. When the Dominicans and Franciscans arrived in China in the 1630s, they launched a bitter attack on their Jesuit rivals. They disputed the Jesuits' tolerance for the Chinese way of life and publicly asserted that Chinese ancestors were burning in hell. Not surprisingly, the emperor reacted angrily, expelling missionaries from China in 1724.

It didn't take long for her enthusiasm to wane. With no training for the board position and naïve to the pockets of power, she found herself sitting quietly, unsure when or if she should speak up. She felt the response to her questions might be that she was "supposed to know"—if not, why was she on the board? She would speak on

Protestants Arrive

The first Protestant missionary in China, Dr. Robert Morrison of the London Missionary Society, arrived in 1807 to respond to the "challenge of Chinese millions." By September 1813, Morrison, assisted by fellow missionary William Milne, had completed translating the New Testament into Chinese. The pair had translated the entire Bible by November 1819. In the second half of the nineteenth century, the opening of the treaty ports brought more missionaries. Christianity grew quickly, with Protestants being dominant. The spread of Christianity during this time period often is associated with the Opium Wars. As described by one historian: "A good many missionaries arrived entangled with the opium trade, sailing above holds stacked with chest on chest of the drug, and generally missions finances were kept afloat by the credit network maintained by the opium merchants—let alone funds which missions received directly from firms connected with the trade..." Source: Diarmaid MacCulloch,

programmatic issues and sometimes was asked her opinion, but overall she didn't feel that her voice mattered.

It may have been my fault for not knowing how to ask and extend myself. There was one other woman, but she didn't attend the board meetings. There were a lot of men, some corporate, and it was hard for me to assert myself.

Christianity: The First Three Thousand Years (Penguin, 2010) 896.

Furthermore, the forced opening of China following the second Opium War and the Unequal Treaty gave missionaries greater freedom in their activities in China's interior. Under intense pressure by the French, who wanted to protect their Catholic missions, the Qing dynasty (1644–1912) included toleration clauses in the Treaty of Tientsin of 1858. The treaty legalized preaching Christianity in China's interior and provided Christians with protection from religious persecution. The Opium Wars also increased interest in all things Western, including Christianity. Protestant work increased drastically following the opening of China, and soon there were 130 Protestant denominations from thirteen countries operating in China, Britain and the United States being the most influential.

The Qing government could not prevent local negative response to Christian missionaries and their influence on the social and political structures of

I really struggled as a board member because I didn't understand what was going on and no one talked me through it, telling me, "This is what we do as a board, and this is how things are; this is where your voice comes in." I really struggled to know my place. I was trying to figure things out and eventually gave up. There was a clear rhythm to how they ran the board meetings. It felt like theater sometimes. Things were predetermined. In times the country. Chief opponents were the Chinese gentry, a class that provided leadership in exchange for privileges in society. White missionaries, protected by treaties, began to exert their influence, serving as advisors on government and military affairs. To convert the Chinese, missionaries established hospitals and schools and provided relief, service traditionally orchestrated by the gentry. Not all those who converted were sincere. The missionaries' benevolence produced "rice Christians"—those who were baptized and attended church as long as missionaries met their physical and social needs. Source: http://history .emory.edu/home/assets/documents/endeavors/ volume2/IanDeeks.pdf

Growing resentment of the West and of Christianity by some segments heightened. The Boxer Rebellion (1899–1901) held foreign imperialism and Christianity as targets. At least thirty-two thousand Chinese Christians and two hundred missionaries were killed by Boxers in the uprising. The Boxer Rebellion was ultimately quashed by the Eight-Nation Alliance of Austria-Hungary, France, Germany, Italy, Japan, Russia, the United Kingdom, and the United States.

of fiscal crisis, I feared, "Oh my God, we're going to shut down!" Then I found out, no, this was part of life in this nonprofit world. I always felt like an outsider. I felt I was there as a token. I never felt like I made any real impact.

Nonetheless, for many Chinese peasants, the Boxers were martyrs—and anti-Western and anti-Christian sentiments grew stronger.

Japan

Missionaries in Japan experienced great success and great failure. Francis Xavier and fellow Jesuits arrived in Japan in 1549, and by the end of the century there were 300,000 Christian converts (MacCulloch, 707). Xavier and fellow Jesuits tried to reach the Japanese on their own terms. Jesuits recruited nearly seventy novices by 1590, concentrating on sons of noblemen and samurai who would command respect. Source: http://en.wikipedia.org/wiki/Francis_Xavier

The monks later realized that Xavier was preaching a rival religion and grew more aggressive toward his attempts at conversion. In its effort to advance, the church soon adopted some extreme methods, including the introduction of Buddhist and Shinto religious elements into Christian worship and using feudal lords to coerce their subjects to convert. The shoguns were also eventually persuaded that Christianity was an attempt to soften them up for European conquest.

It took me a long time to be at ease with a person who is not of color. I am more at ease with a person of color because I don't feel that part of my identity will be dismissed. I think the color piece is higher than gender. I had an African American

Added to that, quarrels among rival missionary groups aggravated the situations, and as a result, as many as 280,000 Japanese Christians were persecuted and thousands were martyred. In 1626, Christianity was banned in Japan, and for the next 250 years, the nation closed its door to the rest of the world. Source: http://us.omf.org/omf/japan/about_japan/christianity_in_japan

During the ban, organized Christianity was persecuted. Believers were hunted, exiled, martyred, or forced to go underground. After the reopening of Japan in the 1850s, biblical Christianity was introduced for the first time. In 1867, foreign missionaries were allowed to enter the country again, and Roman Catholics, Protestants,

male supervisor, who was really a mentor, and the kinds of conversations we would have were so much safer in my mind. I was able to work to a level of achievement that would not have been possible if I was [supervised by] a white person.

Pam's experience implies the need for whites to champion diversity in their organizations. The challenge is to change their styles of operating so others feel comfortable and welcome on boards, in supervisory positions, and while serving in grassroots urban missions. Newcomers must be assured that the power dynamics are changeable and that it is safe to bring problems up. "There's so much work to be done to create structures of support," she states.

and Orthodox missionaries arrived in Japan. In 1880, the Japanese New Testament was published, followed by the Old Testament in 1887. This allowed Christianity to enter without the strong voice of culture and Japanese were able to protect their culture. Source: http://www.christarjapan.org/history.html

For a period, the West was the region to emulate and Christian missionaries were successful again. A change in the government would again limit Christianity. Under the Meiji government (1868–1912), state Shinto and the emperor system created a sense of nationalism, with a shift toward gaining Western knowledge without adopting Christianity. Source: http://jpnreligions.weebly.com/christianity.html

"Christian organizations have so much more work to do than secular organizations when it comes to race. White people come into urban neighborhoods to change it. There's always a question as to who holds the power. There needs to be a change. We don't have choice. It's really hard to have this conversation because I don't think they (whites) get the paternalism and the colonialism and its impact. I think it's sinful; it's awful. It seems unfair that people of color have to always be the ones to speak up. Change will happen when more white allies start talking about this to their contacts."

Pam's voice quickens as she recalls the isolation she felt, the conversations she had to initiate, and the uncomfortable questions she had to raise if, indeed, issues were ever going to be discussed. In sharing her experiences, it was as though she relived the pain of always being the one to speak out, the voice of justice that few wanted to hear.

"I see certain things and everyone else doesn't," she says. "I keep pushing. I felt I had to work a lot harder to be seen as legitimate. It seemed like I had some sort of agenda. People said, 'You keep harping on this issue, and it's going to tear up our group.' That was a struggle because people thought everything that I said came out of that. I spent a lot of time wondering, 'Should I bring this up?'

"When the president of the organization, a white male, said something about the challenges of people of color, everyone listened. Not the same reaction when I said it."

Young, inexperienced, surrounded by powerful white men, Pam let her voice fall silent. One can't help but imagine how the board and her missions team might have blossomed—touched real issues about culture and race—if someone had mentored her and supported her instead of leaving her to wave the banner alone.

Missio Dei means multiethnic boards and top leaders.

The idea that missions are the white man's burden, the domain of whites only to serve, is an old view that has little to do with society today and one that was never of God anyway. When I became the president of a missions organization, I discovered that beneath the surface, many whites hold this belief. However crazy it may sound, this impression is secretly buried in the hearts of some drawn to urban missions. And the higher up the ranks I rose, the more I found it to be true.

I was incredibly well accepted as a person who worked in a program and led people on the ground. But it was a different story when, as president of the organization, the final decisions had to come by my desk and a called meeting needed to have my approval and input. The final confirmations of this belief came in person from "friends" who let me know a black person could not do this job.

Whites in missions need to prayerfully self-examine. Is there an inherent threat that persons of color bring to the table when they sit as equals? Do you feel less needed, displaced even?

I recently visited a new ministry that worked with "poor" kids from the city. The founders were quite pleased with the training they established to help employees deal with "urban" kids. I was saddened. They had established a whole culture for white kids to come work with black kids. The founders didn't make the effort to recruit any people of color from the community served. If they had, they wouldn't have needed such an extensive training program. In fact, leaders of color could have trained the founders.

The problem exists because many white-led organizations hire who they know or whoever applies. White Christian leaders don't know people of color or where to recruit applicants. Living in all-white neighborhoods, worshipping at all-white churches, attending all-white social events, serving on all-white boards, it's all quite normal to them—and if one person in the room is nonwhite, all the better for their consciences. They do not reach beyond their own communities to form friendships and relationships. They only venture beyond their white community for missions.

And while the persistence of white Christian missions leadership is in part due to their insular existence, it sometimes can be traced to a perceived threat from nonwhites. Leaders of color, who know more about the urban missions field, aren't hired because whites want to remain the experts. The expressed reasons are always qualifications, of course, but quality leaders of color are sometimes perceived as a threat to "our way of doing things."

Well-meaning white folks with power and resources but very little knowledge of the community being served won't hire a Jamal, a Morehouse College graduate and excellent leader who has bootstrapped from a challenging background similar to the community to be served. The expressed reason for not bringing him on board will be some missing qualification, but the truth is the Morehouse grad could be perceived as a threat. He would not need "urban leadership training" as do whites with great hearts but no understanding. If a Jamal is hired, the white leader may not be needed for as long. Many whites in urban missions declare they would like to work themselves out of jobs, but very few, even after many years, actually step aside, hire an executive director who is not white, or groom indigenous leadership.

Pam felt silenced in board meetings not because she didn't have anything to contribute and not because the existing board members didn't appreciate her, but because there was not an expressed and realized intention by the board to train and mentor her. No effort was made to restructure a predominantly white culture and make it welcoming to people of color.

From Pam's experience on the board, I learned that people of color have a lot to give and a voice to offer, but need encouragement and training as they navigate places of power, like boardrooms.

How to diversify boards

Diversity in general means a collective of representatives from various races and cultures. That does not necessarily mean the collective is multicultural or multiethnic. Multiculturalism brings into play differences in where people live, economic backgrounds, ethnicity, education, etc. I recently reviewed a conference pamphlet that advertised "a diverse group of national and regional leaders focus on Jesus' Great Commission." While the list of African American, Asian, Hispanic, white, and female conference presenters represented diversity, it did not represent multicultural or multiethnic expression because the style of the conference was monocultural, presented in an Anglo context. The speakers all had the same theological underpinnings. Diversifying a board does not mean bringing aboard folks who don't look alike but are still fully assimilated into the majority culture.

In my experience, the two biggest challenges to the boardroom are Native Americans, who are just silenced because their story has no explanation or excuse, and the African Americans who are loud, boisterous, and outspoken. But the challenge applies to all non-whites. Ra Mendoza, a young Latino leader, said, "I think white people feel attacked when I speak up, give my voice. They have said that to me. Then they stop talking about it."

I often feel I am in the boardroom because I can bridge between a white board and my brother who is Afrocentric. My goal is to have both in the same room and that they appreciate each other. The white board can't see themselves connecting with a person whose language comes from a place of pain and hurt and who does not accept that the status quo is the answer. The Afrocentric board member does not aim for reconciliation because he feels the races are not reconciling. Reconciliation implies that there was once togetherness, but we were never ever together. We are coming together for the first time and must make that happen on new terms. That view scares whites.

To diversify boards the executive director must first understand this and go on a personal learning curve because his or her life motives will be challenged. The executive director must do a personal soul search. He or she will be brought under scrutiny, pushed to break racial codes. Their personal life will be under a microscope. They will put themselves in a lonely position between two worlds for a while, maybe even a long while. Diversity is not highlighting one culture over another. Rather, it saying that if we blend the cultures, we look more like the Creator. The executive director must be in the middle, not on any side, not attached to any one culture. The executive director must drive the initiative to diversify. If the executive director is not fully behind a move toward diversification, the efforts won't be effective.

The next step is making the majority of board members representative of the constituency served. Boards must set a percentage and make this part of the organization's bylaws.

Look for qualified board members of color, not merely tokens. Being part of the constituency group alone does not meet the qualifications for diversity. For example, if your board needs legal expertise, look for a lawyer from the constituency group.

Set up a diversity committee to look at the organization from the top down regarding whether the majority of the board represents the constituency served. Empower that committee to bring recommendations to the main board.

Identify potential board members by going to places in

your constituent community where leadership already exists—neighborhood and other grassroots organizations, small business associations, black colleges, etc.

Make sure the board has a good governance committee—the group that ensures good process, policy, and procedures are followed, adherence to the bylaws. This committee reaches out to potential board candidates. (For example, Christian Community Development Association [CCDA] established a governance committee to establish term limits, policy, and orientation for new board members and a matrix for board balance and diversity by race, gender, practitioner, organizational thinkers, businesspeople.)

The heart of the board

I formed my first board twenty-four years ago for a small nonprofit in Philly. Over the years I have served on many boards. Some were incredible, others quite challenging. In most cases I have met people who for one reason or another cared deeply for the work of the organization they served.

The nation's estimated one and a half million nonprofit organizations range from the wealthiest—the Bill and Melinda Gates Foundation, which has a $38 billion endowment—to tiny ones that care for local community parks for a few hundred dollars. A lot of people volunteer on boards and offer themselves to work on behalf of something about which they care deeply.

When you sign on as a board member you assume responsibility for the stated mission, goals, and financial capacity of an organization. In plain terms: What are we doing? How are we going to get there? Who is going to pay for it? This is not an easy task, whether it's $300 or $3 billion. It takes commitment and care.

Money matters, even in nonprofits. The standard rule of boards is get, give, or get off. This has helped boards with financial concerns. Most boards are constantly figuring out funding, and that is important. But I would like to talk about the heart of the board.

People who care are the central theme of boards. Members care about the work. I have served on about twenty-five boards over the years—Christian, secular, urban, suburban, forty-member boards and four-member boards—and I have rarely attended a passionless board meeting. Boards are full of passion. Accountants are passionate about the audits. Lawyers are passionate about the bylaws, and they are joined by passionate theologians, bankers, artists, and practitioners, all bringing their voices together to pursue the stated mission. The heart of the board is the mission and most board members are passionate about the mission. That's why they serve.

The key ingredient of board membership is belief in action. A board member puts action behind what they believe through participation. Board donors give of their resources to help meet the mission of the organization. Board members give time, contacts, and professional expertise. When a person decides to serve on a board, they make a conscious decision to give because they believe.

The heart of the board is also friendship. From the first board on which I served to my present one at Word Made Flesh, I was valued as a friend. I will be the first to admit that many friendships are strained on boards, but when you look closely, you will see that relationship is why a lot of board members serve. They have a friend who serves or they want to support a friend as the executive director. This relational aspect of board membership is one of deep accountability. Friendships hold members accountable to the mission, vision, and funding of an organization. A good friend is one who can celebrate with you as well as hold you accountable. Such friendship is present in many ways on boards and goes hand in hand with the donor relationship.

Whether or not your board has close bonds, remember that no two boards look alike. You need to find the personality of your board and live in that reality as you move together toward the mission you love. Diverse boards are complicated and messy at times. Fully diversifying your board—not simply providing tokens of color—can be a messy process. But it can be a beautiful transitional period if the true heart of the board is visible: passion, belief, friendship, and accountability.

If your board is missing any of these worthy traits, diversifying can be a wonderful opportunity to deepen your board members' encounters with one another. An organization where these four factors are operative within its board probably has a hardworking executive director and can enjoy the journey to successful diversity.

CHAPTER 7

Fixing Urban Missions Funding

"The majority of younger donors that I know seem to be making decisions more with a business model as opposed to thinking, 'This is the work of the church and how do we support that?' I think people would give more readily to the organization that could present its business model and logic models than to the one that just says, 'This is good work of the church.' I see a shift in funding, which shifts the conversation, too."

—Rob Hughes

E very year, $308 billion is given away in the United States. Of that amount, 85 percent is given by individuals—not corporations, not foundations. In changing missions funding we are talking about reaching people just like us. Your vision, passion, call, vocation, story are vitally important to that individual giving process. If more people involved in missions understood this, they would receive more funding. Asking someone to give is not just about the dollar; it's about creating a space for people to be generous.

It is probably universally understood that money makes the world go around; the more of it you have the better off you are. You can call your own shots, order your own days, and the more money you have, the better you are treated. It is expected that you will have the best seats, first choice, and highest quality if you are high on the economic ladder. This is true even in Christianity. Wealthy Christians may sometimes hide their economic privilege, but it is still there. Our faith doesn't teach us that there is a problem with money. It teaches us there is a problem with privilege based on money. This is the warning given to us:

The Royal Rule of Love

My dear friends, don't let public opinion influence how you live out our glorious, Christ-originated faith. If a man enters your church wearing an expensive suit, and a street person wearing rags comes in right after him, and you say to the man in the suit, "Sit here, sir; this is the best seat in the house!" and either ignore the street person or say, "Better sit here in the back row," haven't you segregated God's children and proved that you are judges who can't be trusted?

Listen, dear friends. Isn't it clear by now that God operates quite differently? He chose the world's down-and-out as the kingdom's first citizens, with full rights and privileges. This kingdom is promised to anyone who loves God. And here you are abusing these same citizens! Isn't it the high and mighty who exploit you, who use the courts to rob you blind? Aren't they the ones who scorn the new name—"Christian"—used in your baptisms?

You do well when you complete the Royal Rule of the Scriptures: "Love others as you love yourself." But if you play up to these so-called important people, you go against the Rule and stand convicted by it.

—James 2:1–8, MSG

It is our work as Christians to make sure we are treating everyone with equality. The Christian community is where people are loved and honored for who they are, not for what they possess. We treat all people with dignity, worth, and respect.

The wall of class

The Pharisees were a class unto themselves. They established themselves as leaders of the church and the Roman governors allowed them to rule as long as they kept some order. They were the "middle class" that pleased Rome and felt themselves to be above the common people of their day. In some ways we Christians continue this tradition with our allegiances to wealth and prosperity, and as long we get our way on issues like prayer in schools or abortion, we remain satisfied and silent. One would think those are the only issues that matter to Christians. We need to knock down the wall of class and swear allegiance to being followers of Jesus only. Wherever we see injustice, we must challenge it at all costs.

We are all praying that one day we will be with the Creator in heaven and for the goal of shalom here on earth. If we are to represent God here on earth, the walls of class must fall. Economic justice must replace class if we are to answer the prayer of Jesus. It can be done. The spirit of God, which moved along the waters and created a world, is in us.

Trina, an African American veteran of urban ministry, made this comment about missions funding:

> Class is a factor. The models that are out there do not encourage people who are not wealthy or don't have a wealthy network. The pervasive model is raise your own support, which assumes that you come from churches or families or a network of people who have a lot of disposable income to share with you; enough so that you could put together a salary for yourself and to support you and your family.
>
> The reality is that either people of color do not have those networks or, for wealthier African Americans, this hasn't been a world they've been exposed to. So they don't understand why you have to raise your own support. They ask, "Why don't they pay you?" The model doesn't making sense to them, so they are not inclined to support in that way.
>
> In its structure, missions is set up in a way that is less inclusive of people of color. We who serve are dependent upon raising funds, and the money is still controlled largely by whites.

How to fix missions funding

Missions funding's two major drivers are personal support and fund-raising by a board. These funding methods depend on having a network of family and friends that has a large amount of discretionary income or relationships with large donors— corporations, foundations, wealthy individuals. This traditional funding model tends to work for upper middle class and wealthy whites who want to serve in missions.

In today's missions service culture, we need to change the funding system.

Expand Relationally

How do we introduce volunteers into networks that will be able to fund them?

Let's take Nicole from the previous chapter. Individual board members needed to have seen it as part of their responsibility to get to know Nicole. Each board member should have invited Nicole to dinner and, during that dinner, gotten to know her driving passion for missions and found out her other missions interests. Then they might have found ways to support those other interests.

Community Investment

How do we create viable business-type models that lessen dependence on personal support?

Discover how the local constituency can invest in the work in ways that lower your expenses. For example, a church with a parsonage can lower its expenses on housing. In Mission Year, we began to talk with congregations that owned houses in the neighborhood. In exchange for allowing Mission Year to use the house for the year, two of our volunteers would work in their after-school programs. This exchange took our budget for housing from $300,000 per year to $20,000 per year. Also, through the exchange, local churches became invested in the program. Mission Year wasn't just coming in and doing good in the neighborhood, the churches and Mission Year were doing good *together*.

Creative Exchange

How do we lessen dependence on volunteers coming into the community to serve rather than the community meeting its own needs?

A good business example is an urban mission in Bangkok. One of the indigenous missions staff learned how to make relish and jellies. She began to sell them at local markets and now makes enough money to support herself in missions work.

In Kolkata, Sari Bari is a business that trains women who chose to leave the sex trade industry, as artisans to create beautiful, hand-made products that are sold online and in other venues. Its ninety employees have employment, health care, and a way to sustain their families. They are no longer vulnerable. (See saribari.com.)

Raise Awareness

Communities of color need to be educated about the "missions industry" and service, especially the impact and availability of vocations in missions. One can have a degree in marketing and work at a nonprofit that is doing Christian work in the world. One can be a filmmaker and create films for nonprofits that are doing good work around the world. You can love sports and coach young people at a Boys and Girls Club. All those can be jobs, even roles to which one is called by God, but in some positions, support is needed.

Raising Support from Communities of Color

Here are ways to make the concept of raising support inviting to people of color.

Whites give as individuals. People of color give via groups, in community—churches, fraternal organizations, etc. Reach out to a gatekeeper in the group—the pastor, the head of the sorority. Have that gatekeeper ask on your behalf. (Pastors remain gatekeepers of giving in communities of color.)

Recognize that communities of color look for direct exchange, how the missions giving ties into their overall objectives and identity. Study the objectives of members of the served community. Don't come in with your own objectives unless you show how they are consistent with those of the served community. Don't assume your missions goals are the same as community goals. Explain how your missions work will affect the community with which the giver is connected. Don't expect giving simply for good deeds.

Asking someone to give is not just about the dollar; it's an invitation to participate in the work of the mission. Ensure those from the served community are invited to participate in meaningful ways other than fund-raising. Reach out via face-to-face meeting rather than relying solely on mail, phone, or social media.

In endeavors where people are not driven by profit, but motivated by how they can do good, the questions still seem to come back to money. If a board can keep its organization focused on vision, vocation, and its mission, then the driver becomes people. Money decisions should always be filtered through people, vision, and vocation. Once those filters are removed, decisions start to be made around money. When that happens—when people are not the major driver of decisions—the decisions are made from corporate structure and knee-jerk financial responses. Boards have to work against that.

The flip side is not to let money drive your mission. Just because you have the money doesn't mean you undertake missions. You do missions because it's part of your vision and vocation, not because you have the money.

CHAPTER 8

Focus on Christ, Not Culture

This chapter is contributed by Mark Charles, a speaker, writer, and consultant from Fort Defiance, Arizona (Navajo Nation).

> "I want to know Jesus as a Native American, not as a white man."
>
> —*Richard Twiss*

When the day of Pentecost came, they were all together in one place. Suddenly a sound like the blowing of a violent wind came from heaven and filled the whole house where they were sitting. They saw what seemed to be tongues of fire that separated and came to rest on each of them. All of them were filled with the Holy Spirit and began to speak in other tongues as the Spirit enabled them.

Now there were staying in Jerusalem God-fearing Jews from every nation under heaven. When they heard this sound, a crowd came together in bewilderment, because each one heard their own language being spoken. Utterly amazed, they asked:

"Aren't all these who are speaking Galileans? Then how is it that each of us hears them in our native language? Parthians, Medes and Elamites; residents of Mesopotamia, Judea and Cappadocia, Pontus and Asia, Phrygia and Pamphylia, Egypt and the parts of Libya near Cyrene; visitors from Rome (both Jews and converts to Judaism); Cretans and Arabs—we hear them declaring the wonders of God in our own tongues!" Amazed and perplexed, they asked one another, "What does this mean?"

—*Acts 2:1–12, NIV*

What does this mean?

It is a basic, even simple question, but one that requires reflection and deep self-awareness in order to be answered well.

After Jesus died and rose to heaven, God had a challenge. He wanted to plant his church. He wanted to let the world know about his Son and the victory over death he had accomplished on the cross. And it so happened that at that exact time Jews from all throughout the world were in Jerusalem. But God had a challenge. They all were fluent in different languages. Sure, many of them probably spoke some Greek or Hebrew. But those languages were, most likely, best understood in translation and were not the heart languages of the people. And because it was God's desire that his bride know him intimately and not in translation, he had to do a miracle. Either he had to allow everyone to be completely fluent in Greek or Hebrew or he had to allow his disciples to speak the languages of the nations. Either option required a miracle. God simply had to choose. Did he want his church to begin with a single common and assimilated language? Or did he want his church to be born reflecting the diversity of his creation and his character?

What does it mean that God chose the latter and allowed his disciples to speak the languages of the nations?

Language is one of the most effective vehicles for passing on and perpetuating culture. If you want to destroy a culture, one of the most efficient methods is to destroy the language. The U.S. government and many Christian churches knew this full well. When they established boarding schools to assimilate Native Americans to Western culture—in an attempt to "Kill the Indian in him, and save the man" (Capt. Richard Henry Pratt)—native students were forbidden from, and even punished for, speaking their language.

Today, many native languages are dying and many more are already dead. But it is telling that as many tribes begin to gain some financial footing, one of their first priorities is to establish programs to restore, teach, and preserve their languages.

Assimilation is <u>not</u> among God's goals for the Church.

Ya'at'eeh abini. My name is Mark Charles, I am born of the Wooden Shoe People and I am born of the Water Flows Together People. My maternal grandfather is also of the Wooden Shoe People and my paternal grandfather is from the Bitter Water Clan. I live with my wife and our three children on the Navajo Reservation, where they attend a *Dine' Bi'Olta*, a Navajo immersion school that teaches the Navajo culture and provides educational instruction in the language of our people.

Nearly fifteen years ago I was called to pastor a church in Denver, Colorado, called the Christian Indian Center. This church was planted about fifty years ago as an outreach to the native peoples of the Denver area. There was a period of about six months between the time I was called and when I was able to move to Denver with my family. During that time I was serving as the leader of the small group ministry at our church in Gallup, New Mexico. That church was predominantly white, but there was also a good mix of Native American and Hispanic members as well.

During this six-month period, God gave me a desire to understand his heart for racial reconciliation. I didn't want to read books or hear sermons on it. I wanted to go straight to the source. So I started a small-group Bible study and we did a survey of the Bible. Beginning in Genesis and going through Revelation, we extracted and examined every passage we could find that had to do with racial reconciliation. This survey took several months, and at the end we collaborated and wrote the following definition: "In obedience to God, racial reconciliation is a commitment to building cross-cultural relationships of forgiveness, repentance, love, and hope that result in 'walking in beauty' with our fellow man and God."

This was really the first time in my life that I realized God's goal for his Church did not include assimilation. At our church, on any given Sunday, you could look out from the pulpit and see diversity of skin color throughout the congregation. But the underlying culture of our church was white American and the language was English. We had a certain style of gathering, preaching, singing, and worshipping, and visitors were extremely welcome to join us. But if they wanted to worship in a different style or hear preaching in a different language, then ours was probably not the church for them. We were an assimilated congregation and small tastes of different cultures were allowed, but the underlying structures and values of our church were reflections of the dominant culture.

Once my eyes were open to our own church, I was shocked to see this underlying value for assimilation at the foundation of a vast majority of churches throughout our country.

What did this mean? And why did God open my eyes and choose to arm me with this definition of racial reconciliation just before sending me off to pastor a Native American congregation?

The answer: contextualized worship

One of my favorite questions to ask students when I lecture in seminaries is "Who has ever attended a contextualized worship service?" Often, one or two hands go up, usually from students with darker color skin.

"Do the rest of you go to church?" I ask.

Heads nod.

"Then I assume that each of you attend Jewish synagogues that meet on Saturday and worship in Hebrew?"

Heads shake.

"No. We attend normal churches. We meet on Sunday and speak English," they respond.

"Well, guess what?" I inform them. "You all attend highly contextualized worship services."

If Jesus were to walk into almost any church service in the United States, he would definitely be confused and probably ask questions like:

Missionaries to Native Americans

Missionaries took the Gospel and their cultural interpretations of it to Native Americans. The Massachusetts Bay Colony charter—its colonial seal featured a picture of a Native American uttering the words "Come over and help us"—perpetuated the fantasy that Native Americans invited Europeans to North America and needed their help and guidance. Conflict among the Puritans and natives arose, despite the fact that the early European settlers survived the first winter only because the Native Americans extended food, shelter, and knowledge to them. Christian acts of compassion were extended during the early interactions between the natives and missionaries, and the indigenous of the land were the ones performing them.

Efforts to reach Native Americans with Christianity began early. In 1663, the Eliot Bible was published in Cambridge, Massachusetts, under the title *The Holy*

1. "Why do you meet on Sunday?"
2. "Why does your pastor stand elevated and behind a pulpit?"
3. "Why is the sermon preached in English and has three points?"
4. "Why are your services only seventy-five minutes in length and always dismissed before the start of the football game?"

Bible Containing the Old Testament and the New. Translated into the Indian Language. Translated into Algonquian by John Eliot, "apostle to the Indians," it was used to support his missionary efforts among Native Americans. The Eliot Bible appeared some 120 years before the first complete English edition of the Bible was published in the United States. Source: http://www.loc.gov/exhibits/treasures/trm036.html

Overall, Native Americans resisted Christian conversion. For them, accepting Christianity generally involved giving up their language, severing kinship ties with natives who had not been "saved," and abandoning their traditional homes to live in European-style "praying towns." Puritan-Indian relations were further troubled by recurring disagreements over land use and land rights. The notion of private property was foreign to Native Americans, who viewed selling land as sharing land with new groups.

In 1810, Protestants established the interdenominational American Board of Commissioners for Foreign

Nearly every Christian worship service in the United States is highly contextualized and has been adapted to make sense for the culture, worldview, time perception, and values of Western European/American culture. This is not a bad thing.

If you look closely at the model of Jesus and see him first, you will not see a Jew, but a God who came to earth to restore

Missions (ABCFM), America's first foreign missionary society. Missions to Native Americans began in 1817 with a mission station in Brainerd, Tennessee, to serve the Cherokees. In 1819, Congress established a "civilization fund," appropriating $10,000 annually to support

relationship with his creation. Then his teaching style is incredibly contextual and it begins to make sense why he so often spoke in parables and used phrases such as "the kingdom of God is like…"

Jesus was not proclaiming the truths of Jewish culture; instead, he was using the culture, context, and language of the people to help them understand the truths of the kingdom of God. I cannot believe that if the Jews dwelled in the Amazon Basin and lived in huts built on stilts that were sunk deep into the ground to provide a sturdy foundation, Jesus would have told a parable stating, "The wise man built his house upon the rock and the foolish built his house upon the sand." No, he would have told that parable probably in the same way it is told in the Bible translated for the Motilone people—that the wise man built his house on the sand, and the foolish man built his house upon the rock! The truth is not that God or scripture is a rock. The truth is that God and his words are trustworthy, sturdy, and provide a firm foundation. The rock part is merely a contextualized metaphor used to convey this truth to people who happened to live in the desert.

The Christians of Western Europe understood this, which is why they felt free to change their day of worship from Saturday to Sunday. It is also why they use instruments like the piano, organ, guitar, drums, and electronic keyboards to accompany their singing.

assimilation programs for Native Americans. Missionaries, spiritually motivated by the Second Great Awakening and partially supported by federal funds, flocked to Indian country. Source: http://plainshumanities.unl.edu/encyclopedia/doc/egp.rel.027

But unfortunately, what happened historically is that the churches and people of Western Europe contextualized Christian worship for their culture and languages. But then, because their leaders and even their empires were "Christian," they ceased to follow the teachings of Jesus to radically serve the least and love others into the kingdom of God. Instead, they used the model of the Old Testament story of Israel to destroy, subjugate, and assimilate others into their church, which often was indistinguishable from their empire.

Christian empire

This is what happened in the Middle East, Africa, Australia, and of course, the United States and Canada.

When the first Europeans landed on the shores of Central America they were heavily armed, not only with physical weapons, but also with a Doctrine of Discovery. This doctrine originated from a series of papal bulls written in the 1400s. It came out of the Catholic Church, but was quickly adopted by the Protestant church. It stated that any lands that the "Christian" empires of Europe happened to encounter that were not governed by Christian rulers were theirs for the taking. It was this doctrine that gave explorers like Christopher Columbus the incredible arrogance it took to get lost at sea, land on a continent inhabited by millions, and then claim to have discovered it. He was not here as a member of the body of Christ to share the love of Jesus and grow the kingdom of God. Rather, he arrived as a subject of the kingdom of Spain to enrich himself and expand the empire of his rulers.

This is why our nation is built on many incredible-seeming contradictions. As a country, we often point to these words as evidence that at our core, our nation is good and our citizens are just: "We hold these truths to be self-evident, that all men are created equal, that they are endowed, by their Creator, with certain unalienable rights, that among them are life, liberty and the pursuit of happiness."

However, we almost never wrestle with the question "To whom does *all men* actually refer?" Did the authors of the Declaration of Independence truly believe *all* humans were created equal? Fortunately, they give us their definition for this term just twelve short years later, when many of the same men penned another foundational document for the new country they were establishing. The Constitution of the United States of America makes it very clear that "all men" did not refer to women, enslaved Africans, or Native Americans.

Contextual to the poor, prophetic to the rich

Throughout his earthly ministry, Jesus made a pattern of doing everything he could to be contextual to the poor.

Jesus was the Son of God and could have come in any human form; he came as a Palestinian Jew oppressed by the Roman Empire.

He could have been born anywhere. He chose a lowly manger in a barn.

He could have been born into any family he wanted. He chose the stigma of being born out of wedlock to a working-class family in Nazareth.

He could have laid his head on any pillow he wanted. He chose a rock.

He could have called disciples from any segment of society. He chose working-class fishermen and outcast tax collectors.

He could have been made king. He chose to walk away from earthly power.

He could have called Elijah, Moses, or even his Father in heaven to rescue him from death. Instead, he chose to die—humiliated, beaten, naked, and alone—on a cross, along with common thieves and robbers.

Throughout his life, Jesus was presented with choices. And time after time, he chose to humble himself and identify with the poor, the least, and the forgotten.

Jesus came for all people. He did not love any one more than another. But he did have different methods of interacting. To the poor he was contextual, but to the rich Jesus spoke like a prophet. This is most clearly seen in his interaction with the rich young ruler. Here was an outstanding young man who wanted to follow Jesus and inherit eternal life! Very matter-of-factly Jesus told him what was required— sell his possessions, give the money to the poor, and then come and follow him. But Mark 10:22 (NIV) explains, "At this the man's face fell. He went away sad, because he had great wealth."

Native American Removal and Christian Schools

As states formed and Americans moved westward, the "savage" Native American stood in the way. The 1831 Indian Removal Act pushed the native population off their lands and westward. The U.S. government would follow with a full enculturation program. In 1870, Congress authorized an annual appropriation of $100,000 "for the support of industrial and other schools among tribes otherwise not provided for..." The facilities involved were run by churches and missionary societies. Attendance at mission-run schools was mandatory on many reservations for youth ages six to sixteen. Speaking any language other than English was prohibited, as was the practice of native spiritual rites.

Separation of church and state seemingly did not apply when it came to Christianizing Native Americans. In the 1890s, the U.S. government, in the name of the Office of Indian Affairs, stipulated that students in

To me, this is one of the most amazing demonstrations of Jesus's faith and willpower, for he did not stop the man. Upon seeing the young man turn and walk away, Jesus did not call out, "Wait, you don't understand. I didn't mean you had to actually sell your possessions. I just want to hear that you are willing to do so. Besides, I have an 'advisory discipleship group' that you can join.

government schools were to be encouraged to attend church and Sunday school. The reformers, the government, and society in general knew Christianity was essential for the development of the "good Indian." The government mind and the Christian mind were in fact one. Church and state shamelessly walked hand in hand.

Consequently, "Christian proselytizing suffused the educational effort during these decades. Missionaries, of course, attempted to indoctrinate denominational creeds into young Indians. But even as the government edged the mission societies to the margin, its teachers also sought to imbue pupils with some form of Christianity. For most secular as well as missionary educators, 'civilization' was inconceivable unless grounded in Christian—especially Protestant—values." This gross misrepresentation of the *Missio Dei* has associated "Christianity" with pain and conquest instead of love and justice. This is not Christianity. It is sin. It is wrong and should not be celebrated. Source: http://www .twofrog.com/rezsch.html

It only requires four days a month, and if you commit to making regular financial contributions to my ministry, you can keep your possessions. Does this sound like a good fit for you and your schedule? Let's do lunch at that quaint falafel place near the temple next week. We can discuss some other ideas I have for your involvement and investment in this work."

Power vs. authority

Unfortunately most churches and the Christians who attend them are neither contextual to the poor nor prophetic to the rich. Our primary Gospel is not Jesus's death on the cross as found in the Gospels, but rather conquering the promised land by the people of Israel, as found in Joshua. And if we understand the church to be an extension of our "Christian" empire, then it is much more likely that we will be prophetic to the poor and contextual to the rich. Empires are built on power. And power comes from the rich. Therefore the rich and their resources are a necessary part of the empire, the church, and the ministry. But it is nearly impossible to be prophetic to someone upon whom your ministry and livelihood depend.

Power is the ability to act. Authority is the right of jurisdiction.

Early in his ministry Jesus was in the synagogue teaching and people were amazed. "For he taught them as one who had authority, and not as the teachers of the law." (Matthew 7:29) Later, in the same synagogue, a man with an unclean spirit confronted Jesus. The Messiah spoke sternly, commanding the spirit to come out of him. Again the people were amazed and wondered, "What is this? A new teaching—and with authority! He even gives orders to evil spirits and they obey him." (Luke 4:36)

In Mark 4 (NIV), Jesus is asleep at the front of the boat when it begins to sink because of a storm on the waters. The disciples, many of them experienced fishermen, wake Jesus, expecting him to grab a bucket. Instead he stands up, rebukes the wind, and says to the waves, "Quiet! Be still." And the waters became completely calm. The disciples were terrified, not of the perils of the storm, but rather of Jesus's authority. For they ask, "Who is this? Even the wind and the waves obey him!"

For power to be effective it must be demonstrated. Authority is inherent and needs to be exercised.

Jesus was not big on demonstrations. In fact, many times people really had to be on their toes to catch his miracles.

If you were a guest at the wedding at Cana (John 2), you had no idea where the delicious wine came from toward the end of the party. You likely just concluded that your hosts were incredibly extravagant.

If you were one of the professional mourners outside of Jairus's house (Mark 5), you did not witness a miracle, but instead walked home feeling like an idiot because you couldn't tell the difference between a dead girl and a sleeping one!

Throughout the Gospels the religious leaders were constantly asking Jesus to prove his divinity by demonstrating a miracle. But he continually rebuffed them, saying things like, "Truly I tell you, no sign will be given..." (Mark 8, NIV).

You can have power without ever having authority.

In John 19 (NIV), Pilate, frustrated with Jesus's lack of cooperation, tries to scare him with his power by saying, "Do you refuse to speak to me? Don't you realize I have power either to free you or to crucify you?"

Undaunted, Jesus calmly reminds Pilate that while he has power, he lacks authority. Jesus says, "You would have no power over me if it were not given to you from above."

But being given right of jurisdiction is almost always followed with an opportunity to act.

In Mark 6 (NIV), Jesus gives authority to his disciples. A few passages later, he has finished teaching and the people are hungry, but they are in a remote location with nowhere to buy food. Jesus looks at his disciples and instructs them, "You give them something to eat." They don't get it. They throw up their hands in exasperation, complaining they do not have enough power (money) to help the people. Jesus then takes the little they do have, five loaves and two fish, thanks God for it, and begins passing it out. Miraculously, there is more than enough. And then to demonstrate that they missed an opportunity to exercise their authority, Jesus has each of them pick up a basket full of leftover food scraps.

Time perception

Living on the Navajo Reservation gives me an opportunity to observe and work alongside many churches. Every year hundreds, if not thousands, of missionaries come to our land on summer mission trips. Frequently, I am asked to speak with groups and provide an orientation to our land, people, and culture. One of the primary topics I discuss is time perception. The Western perception of time is linear and has strict start and end points. As you move across the time line, events and milestones are passed. Once an event is passed, it is complete and cannot be revisited. This causes a fear of missing something.

So to address this fear, life is organized through the creation of a schedule. This schedule can cover a day—breakfast at seven in the morning, lunch at noon, and dinner at five in the evening. Or it can cover a lifetime—graduate high school by age eighteen, college by age twenty-three, and be established in your career by age thirty. Value and importance are communicated through the honoring of the schedule. So your teacher knows you honor the class because you turn your work in on time. Your boss knows you honor the job because you show up to work on time. Your significant other knows you honor the relationship because you remember key dates and anniversaries. Even God knows that you love him because you arrive to church on time and accommodate time to worship him in your schedule. God, in turn, expresses his concern for you by dismissing Sunday's worship service before the start of the game during football season.

Likewise, offense is communicated when the schedule is not honored. If you show up to a first date two hours late, more than likely there will not be a second date. Or if a newlywed forgets the anniversary of their wedding or his spouse's birthday, that night he will quickly be introduced to the couch in the living room. This is because in a linear perception of time, arriving late or not remembering an event communicates that you were preoccupied with something else more important.

The Navajo perception of time is circular. As you travel around the circle, events and milestones are passed. But if something is missed, very little tension is felt. This is because there is an inherent belief that the event or milestone will come back around again. Navajo life is not organized through a schedule, but rather through the completion of tasks and the concluding of events. Value and importance are communicated by staying until the interaction is over or the task is complete. So here on our reservation, I can make plans to meet an elder for lunch at 1:00 p.m., and even if I show up an hour late, I have not committed an offense. But if I sit down to eat and after thirty minutes look at my watch and explain that I need to leave, that is offensive because I am not allowing the interaction to come to a natural completion.

Time perception is tricky. Over the years I have learned that most people do not think they have a "time perception," but rather they believe they have a "time truth." The problem with that is we tend to judge others by what we understand the "truth" of time to be. I am sure there are many missions teams who have left our reservation having concluded that we Navajos do not care for or love God very much. For we arrived late to every revival service they held and every church service they planned. But I also know that we Navajos have stood shaking our heads as many missions teams drove away, commenting to ourselves how strange it was that they talked constantly about how much they loved God and desired to do his work. Despite their talk, they were always running off to their next scheduled event just as God was showing up at the current one.

I often conclude this teaching by pointing out to the missions teams that throughout the course of their visit to our reservation they will be presented with many lose-lose situations. They will be visiting with a Navajo family and the interaction will go long and they will be forced to make a decision that will offend someone. They can offend the Navajo family by cutting the conversation short so they can run off to the next scheduled event with their team. Or they can offend their teammates by arriving late to, or even missing, their next scheduled event because they stayed and finished their interaction with their Navajo hosts. I tell them, "You need to make the decision now, that when that moment arrives, you will choose to honor your Navajo hosts and offend your teammates. You can reconcile with them on your way home. You are not here to assimilate us to American culture. Nor are you here to demonstrate your power or to expand your Christian empire. You are here to contextualize the Gospel for the Navajo people. You are here to experience the vastness of God's character and the discomfort that comes from the diversity of his body.

You are here to learn what it means that God allowed his disciples to speak the languages of the nations.

CHAPTER 9

Caring for the Stranger: Response to Undocumented Immigrants

"If God is concerned about justice, if God is concerned about equity, if God is concerned about impoverished people, we need to look at places where evangelicals may not consider God will show up. We have to look at Cesar Chavez and that movement and what God did with the Latino movement on the West side. We have to listen to the voices of those who articulated their arguments and realize God set them up in phenomenal ways to influence us."

—*Jimmy McGee*

The population in many urban centers is changing from white to black to brown. The stranger and his family come seeking a better life through work and education. He comes in the dark of night, hiding in vans, crossing rivers on make-shift rafts. If discovered, he is rounded up and incarcerated. Who among us visits him? Counsels him? Fights for his human rights? Who welcomes the stranger or cares for the "certain man beaten and left for dead on the side of the road" as in the parable of the Good Samaritan?

To some Christians, religion and politics should remain separate. To others, Christian tenets and conservative politics go hand in hand. Undocumented immigrants remains a hot-button topic. What should be the Christian response? Are we obliged to obey the law and thwart the efforts of those who would illegally cross borders?

When our missions focus is on Christ, not culture, we are able to pull the immigration issue out of the political realm. When someone truly committed to the *Missio Dei* thinks about immigration, they think about a person. They see people and God's heart for people. They make decisions based not on what we hear from politicians, but rather on the *Missio Dei*. God definitely has a heart for the stranger, the outcast, the wanderer. We know this based on scripture. So much of scripture is God reaching for people outside the structures of the elite. Jesus focused on the people on the outside; he drew attention to them. That's the story of scripture.

As discussed in chapter 1, God wants to know us and for us to know each other. Caring for an undocumented immigrant should be a given. For Christians, nothing in the debate on this issue suggests anything but hospitality. The heart of God deeply connects to the outsider. It is evident from scripture that as followers of Jesus we should be concerned with the person sitting on the fringes. Our hearts must peer out the doors of our churches to see who is not welcome in our larger community, and we must usher that person into the center of our lives. A faith that does not practice justice is a faith void of the presence of Jesus. There is no way to look at his life and justify the treatment of the immigrant in our midst. Politics and laws lose their usefulness when humanity is violated. Christians never have permission to take away rights based on human code. Our call is to uphold justice, grace, and peace, even if the cost is our very lives, just as it cost Jesus his.

Anton Flores, who is of Puerto Rican descent, is cofounder of Alterna, a shared living community of U.S. citizens and immigrants from Latin America committed to acts of mercy, advocacy, and hospitality toward immigrants from Mexico and Guatemala. He challenges the church for remaining silent or coldly indifferent to those entering the United States illegally. Alterna is a network of five houses where everyone lives interdependently, shares meals, and celebrates life. It is a welcoming community, as Anton describes. It is an experiment in Christian missional living and welcoming the stranger.

He advocates changing immigration laws, which he views as unjust, and transforming unjust systems. Anton walked away from a tenure-track position at LaGrange College in southwest Georgia to help undocumented persons from Latin America find housing and ways to make a living. His work is unpaid, but it was a calling he couldn't ignore. It has given him insight on how Christians should serve others if missions are to be effective in cross-cultural contexts. Slightly built, alert, and driven, Anton's intensity is tempered by his compassion for the oppressed. He speaks and acts as though time is running out. And for many undocumented immigrants whom he serves, it just may be.

His day is filled helping immigrants. He is their advocate, assisting them on legal, health, and housing issues. He has seen many hardworking immigrants from Guatemala and Mexico picked up by the police and detained, even known a pregnant woman who gave birth while in detention. She had no one to phone; no one visited her. Her jailers told Anton that he had twenty-four hours to pick up the newborn. Another woman detained was a mother of five. Anton often scrambles to find foster homes or anyone who will take in the children of detained immigrants. Even as the children reach maturity, they remain vulnerable. Anton shared the story about an immigrant whose parents brought him to the United States as a child:

He grew up here, attended high school, married, started a business, and had a family. One day he was pulled over for running a yellow light. The police turned him over to immigration and customs, and he was held in a detention center eighty miles from his family. When I visited him, he broke down in tears, telling me his story.

"Often churches ask, 'What are we to do?' They say, 'The law is the law.' I remind them that we should fight unjust laws just as so many did during the civil rights struggle. We can turn the rule of law into the rule of love, acceptance, and welcome. When policies need to change, the most effective change can be made with our feet and our relationships. We need to be entrenched in love for those who are marginalized."

Anton's guiding principle is simple: "We should love as Christ loved."

Anton's faith leads him to help those who are undocumented, those who are picked up for breaking what he sees as unjust immigration laws.

When Georgia needed construction workers for the 1996 Olympics, undocumented immigrants were welcomed. Hispanic immigrants were heavily recruited for construction projects.

They took all the risks, crossing the border, working without legal papers, while officials looked the other way. After the Olympics, many moved to work in the textile mills in southwest Georgia. Now they are hunted down, pulled over, and imprisoned. Their labor is no longer needed. They are declared illegal and deemed criminals. Where is the church? Where is the missionary work? The church—Christians—look the other way.

We lose our theology when the poor are marginalized, are dehumanized. We permit economic and political violence against them without question. The new wave immigrants become a nameless, faceless group. We forget that all whites in the United States—no matter how elite—are descended from immigrants. The new immigrants are viewed differently than the ancestral immigrants.

Churches that have reached out to the immigrant community are more concerned with increasing their mission numbers than actually changing laws and systems that deem these people "illegals." The mind-set is "if we evangelize them here, they can carry the Gospel to Guatemala." They never talk about immigration laws or challenging them.

Helping the Hispanic population adjust is crucial. How do you minister to someone who is absent from family, from spouse, and finds themselves seeking companionship?

Many have been picked up by the police for driving without a license. But how can they get to work without driving? How can they come to church without driving? Yet they can't get a driver's license without the proper immigration papers. They ask me, "Am I sinning? Do I buy papers on the black market?"

Latinos are treated differently by church leaders and some residents. When Kia Motors came to town and brought jobs,

Early Enslavement and Conversion in Central America

The earliest worldwide importation of the Christian faith outside of continental Europe occurred in the Canary Islands off the coast of Africa. The indigenous were subdued first by the Spaniards and later by the Portuguese, both on a crusade blessed by the pope. Conquest was twofold: souls for the Catholic faith, land for the empire. Franciscans spoke out against enslaving native people who had converted to Christianity, and some opposed enslaving those who had not converted. Yet enslavement would emerge as a secondary concern. By the sixteenth century most of the native population had succumbed to European diseases.

Similar was the fate of the native people of present-day Cuba, Haiti, the Dominican Republic, Puerto Rico, and the Bahamas. In 1513 the Spaniards made clear their intention for the indigenous population, their land, and their religion. The Spaniards issued the Requirement (read to the natives in Spanish, which few natives understood). The Requirement gave this

there were signs in yards that read, "Thank you Jesus for Kia." A banner in front of the prominent church written in English and Korean read: "God Loves You and Our Church Welcomes You." But the Hispanic population has not gotten the same welcome.

ominous warning: "If you do not do this, however, or resort maliciously to delay, we warn you that, with the aid of God, we will enter your land against you with force and will make war in every place and by every means we can and are able, and we will then subject you to the yoke and authority of the Church and Their Highnesses." Source: http://www.doctrineofdiscovery.org/requerimiento.htm

Maya of the Yucatán of present-day southern Mexico, Guatemala, and western Honduras also suffered greatly. Conquerors and missionaries in great ships arrived in the area bringing destruction, cultural annihilation, and a new religion. Even when clergy found similar analogies between Aztec religion and Christian practices (such as the sign of the cross and belief in virgin birth), they responded negatively as if such were blasphemy. Clergy hardened their tolerance of indigenous religious practices. In 1541 and 1546, the Maya of the Yucatán rebelled against all things Spanish, including Catholicism, and were brutally crushed. In 1562, Franciscan missionaries in the Yucatán discovered that some indigenous converts secretly continued to practice their religious rites and made mockery and satire of

When one of the churches tore down its old sanctuary and built a new one, they used Latino labor, yet Latinos are not welcomed as the Koreans, who brought capital. Christians need to open their eyes to see how the 'stranger' is being treated.

Red, Brown, Yellow, Black, White

> Holy Week. In response, the Franciscan provincial Diego de Landa set up inquisitions and unleashed a campaign of interrogation and torture. Spanish clergy altered their views of the indigenous, rarely trusting them with sacred Christian roles. Indigenous people could become assistants in the liturgy, but never principals—catechists, sacristans, cantors, and instrumentalists, but not priests. This practice of allowing even those who converted to serve but not take on major roles is what we still fight today as we see many people of color working in missions. When it comes to boardrooms and CEO positions, people of color are excluded from these. Source: Diarmaid MacCulloch, *Christianity: The First Three Thousand Years* (New York, NY: Viking Press, 2009), 700.

Churches want to spread the Gospel for the sake of the Gospel, but not always to assist those whom they are serving. Do churches want to increase their numbers or make a difference in the lives of those in need?

His challenge extends beyond his quiet midsized southern town to the heart of the state's economic urban hub, Atlanta. Anton has organized pilgrimages, often bringing discomfort to the conservative religious structure during the holiest of Christian seasons.

The Holy Week Pilgrimage for Immigrants is an act of faith, solidarity, and hospitality. It is a prayer with feet. With our

Clergy who tried to protect the indigenous were limited in their success. In 1512, the Laws of Burgos, a result of Dominican and Franciscan friars protesting the ill treatment of the indigenous populations of the island of Hispaniola, outlined humane treatment of the natives and how to convert the population to Catholicism. Yet even these laws failed to truly protect the native people. Under the laws, indigenous people were relocated to communities under the watchful eye of an overseer who would construct a church and ensure the natives learned and practiced the tenets of the Catholic Church—even against their will. Holy men, even if they tried, were powerless to protect them. Christianity, the indigenous found, was backed by military power of an earthly king.

feet we pray that our faith communities and nation will search for ways that favor a spirit of solidarity with and justice for immigrants. We walk by a faith that transcends borders and bids us to overcome all forms of discrimination and violence so that we may build relationships that are just and loving. The challenge to the church is to humanize Jesus, the God who took on human flesh.

Christ calls us to love our neighbor. Matthew 25 tells us, "When I was hungry, you gave me meat. When I was thirsty, you gave me drink, when I was a stranger you took me in. When I was in prison you came and visited me." Christians are to come visit the Jesus who is detained and facing deportation, come see the Jesus who often visits us as an unauthorized immigrant from Latin America. Jesus told us, "As you have done it unto the least of these, you have done it unto me."

Psalm 91:1–6 (NIV) is applicable to missions ministries for immigrants. We have to create the safe place, the shelter of God, for them. When the immigrant comes into contact with Christian missions, when they see us, they see that safe place, that shelter of God.

Whoever dwells in the shelter of the Most High
will rest in the shadow of the Almighty.
I will say of the Lord, "He is my refuge and my fortress,
my God, in whom I trust."
Surely he will save you
from the fowler's snare
and from the deadly pestilence.
He will cover you with his feathers,
and under his wings you will find refuge;
his faithfulness will be your shield and rampart.
You will not fear the terror of night,
nor the arrow that flies by day,
nor the pestilence that stalks in the darkness,
nor the plague that destroys at midday.

CHAPTER 10

Who God Called to the Urban Missions Landscape

"I know what those conversations are like: Is he articulate enough for us? Does he represent our ideas enough? Is he too much to the right or to the left? Will he fit in places that will allow us to get more funding, or will he unhinge opportunities that we have? These are frightening conversations."

—Jimmy McGee

The urban missions landscape is dominated—at least in numbers, although not in effectiveness—by well-meaning groups led by whites, and the common explanation is "Not many people of color are interested in this work" or "We don't know of any people of color who will join us." The inner city has long been a place where racial stereotypes, Christian missions, and bigotry converge, oftentimes in one organization or group.

Alice is a quiet, very observant African American woman. If you ask her to speak her mind, she will—forthrightly, no apologies. She was one of the founders of a private Christian school. However, the board chair (a white male) is credited with establishing the school, despite her enormous contributions. Parents and teachers viewed her as the leader, as she was their primary contact. Unfortunately, the majority of the board—especially a key white donor whose gifts made a difference—did not.

I don't feel I was ever acknowledged by the board as the real leader of the school," says Alice.

> I completed all the documents, hired staff, did everything but fund-raising to get the school established. I was acting principal when the school started and for the first few years. Then I was moved to another position, and they hired another woman with more "credentials" to be principal. When the person hired didn't work out and quit, it was my expectation that I'd be asked to serve as interim principal. I don't think the board recognized all that I did, and some of that had to do with my race.

"It may have been my work style." She acknowledges the perception of the board and many white people toward black women. "I've been told, 'People are intimidated by you. People are afraid to approach you or to say things to you. People were uncomfortable or unsure how to address you.' I feel like they are seeing me through their own mean-African-American-woman stereotype."

Alice's experience coming to the South was that people were surprised she was in the leadership position. As a black woman with a forthright manner, just being herself made others uncomfortable.

When Alice made the decision to move on, she sensed that the board breathed a sigh of relief.

> They didn't know what to do with me. The students and parents saw me as the leader. The board didn't have cause to get rid of me, and it would have made them look bad. They didn't know how to handle it. Walking away from the school wasn't easy. I felt like I put everything that I *was* into the school. But the board and I were going in two different directions.

Direction is shaped by perception. Missions programs shaped by leaders from outside the community served invariably will look different from those shaped by persons from that community or connected to it by heritage. The view from the inside out is different from the outside-in perspective. By insisting on their own direction and believing that funding determines decision making, whites have usurped the role of God. They "call" those they trust and with whom they are comfortable to positions of leadership and may fail to support those whom God has called.

Alice has been a principal, has created children's programs for many years, and now does training for organizations targeting urban kids. She asks those already working with kids of color what they think of when they think of "urban" and what they think of the phrase "urban kids." The list of responses is overwhelmingly negative. Those who want to make a difference still have extremely judgmental images of the city and the young people who live there. Missionaries who hold such views must ask themselves whether they are truly able to help those to whom they feel called.

Missionaries must emerge from the served community.

Alice believes racist perceptions in missions prevent us from together accomplishing the *Missio Dei* and keep programs from being all they can be. She also believes that the black church has some responsibility to urge black Christians to respond to God's call for urban missionaries. "Those who are coming into the city to do service and mission trips tend to be almost all white. So kids of color do not see people who look like them coming to help and to serve people. And they don't think that it's their own responsibility to serve the less fortunate in their own community. That's a big problem on our side."

The scant number of African Americans in urban missions work, hence the perception that it is work for whites, goes back to funding.

"We have to have other funding possibilities," continues Alice.

The African American church has to engage in missions outside of itself. It tends to be inner focused and less inclined to give outside of its own missions organizations. It must teach its young people and send them to serve. To encourage people of color to give, they have to have seats at the table in Christian organizations and structures. These organizations must begin to think, "How can we include people who look different from us? Latinos, Asians, African Americans, Native Americans, across the leadership structure from board level all the way down?" There has to be a conversation and deliberate action to bring people into the organizations. That's going to make every organization better.

Any organization that is operating from one people's point of view is very limited and does not display the full glory of God. God is not one-dimensional. The Almighty deliberately self-revealed to all these groups of people. We're giving a very slanted view of God to the world, only reflecting a limited part of our Lord. That limits everything else we do. As much as we do that is great and wonderful, how much more could we do if we would come together and everybody saw that we all had a role?

When minorities leave your organization, consider it a red flag.

Grace is senior director at a social justice organization. It's a position she's held for several years. She is proud of the agency's work and its legacy of advocacy.

She is well suited for the leadership position in the organization, but her climb to this position had its difficult seasons. She served as a volunteer in other organizations and as a staff worker on a campus ministry. As a student, she came to the campus ministry full of fire, eager to make a difference, ready to confront issues of race and of culture.

The campus at the time was 60 percent Asian American. The next largest majority was white, then African American. We as a community made a commitment to move forward on issues of racial reconciliation. Because of that commitment, I can say my experiences were gratifying, but they also were painful. There were lots of lessons learned by the community.

When I first got there, in my mind I could hear the voice of Jesse Jackson ringing in my ear: "You are somebody. Don't silence your voice. You have something to say. Speak up! Be heard. Lead. Challenge. Ask questions. Question things!" I think it's one of the hallmarks of African American culture that since slavery, we've developed a culture where we speak our minds. We don't mince words. In the Northeast where I grew up, that's how it was in our neighborhoods.

When I got to the campus ministry, I would raise my hand in the group, express an opinion, and ask what about this, what about that? I had a really revealing and helpful conversation with my roommate, who was a Korean American woman. She had interpreted my raising my hand as arrogance, because I was not the oldest person in the room. In the Asian culture she had experienced, you show deference to those who are older and to those in greater authority, so you don't assume you know more than those who are older. The pervasive opinion on the team became "Grace is arrogant, Grace is opinionated." That's how I was labeled.

Another black staff person from a sister campus ministry talked with the group and explained that Grace was asking questions and speaking her mind, which is to be expected in the African American culture.

That was a cultural clash. When we judge others through our lenses, it's as if our culture has a lock on what is true or right. Those are the things—the little things—that wear down the constitution of minorities. It's usually not the big explosive things. But the unnamed culture clashes. People don't usually have those conversations like the one where my Korean sister told me what she really thought and why. People divide. They don't trust each other. They whisper behind each other's backs. That's the norm. I was blessed to have that conversation with my Korean sister and she was blessed, too.

She eventually resigned her position as director of racial reconciliation at the campus ministry when she was turned down for a position as an area director in the organization. Candidates were required to take an assessment that measured leadership skills, the ability to manage others and administer budgets.

The tool determined I was an 86 percent match for the area director position. That's a high match. My supervisor said, "I don't believe it." That's what he said in response to my high score on his own hiring tool: "I don't believe it." He offered me a lower position. I reviewed with him the documentation from the assessment tool, the charts, the written comments on my skills and abilities. He looked at it and offered, "How about we make you a team leader of a small staff team on a new campus where we are just starting?"

She's quiet as she remembers the incident. "I said, 'Thank you for making it easy for me to leave.' And I left. "

How many Graces have left your organization? What should have been done in this situation?

Before your organization loses any people of color—or hires any—ask yourself: "Is it more important for our organization to have a culture that assimilates others or to have varying voices that bring different perspectives?" In many cases the answer is assimilation; white culture will welcome nonwhites as long as the newcomers, the people of color, go with the status quo. Examine your own feelings honestly. Review the actions that moved you to hire the person for the position. Was their ethnicity viewed as a welcomed benefit to your organization because it would provide a fresh perspective? Or was their ethnicity seen as simply a different package on the same ideas and cultural values you hold? The latter leaves many leaders, especially leaders of color who have a different cultural lens, on the outside looking in.

Leaders of color in your organization will face a difficult situation in their work and their call. If they speak out they risk being misunderstood, being perceived as a troublemaker or as someone who is trying to sow division. In reality, they are not looking to cause division; rather, they are speaking from their cultural perspective. Leaders of color who remain silent and keep their cultural insights to themselves are forced to live a double life, and many will eventually quit. And your organization loses the valuable insight they could offer.

If Grace's boss had been willing to examine his own potentially racist thinking and then sit down with her and listen to her perspective, he might have learned that she was a bridge builder, bringing a perspective that was missing from the organization. Understanding this would have enhanced his work tremendously. Instead, he caused a breakdown of trust and reinforced stereotypes. And he lost a great leader. He had to begin again with a new employee, at a loss of valuable time.

If a leader of color leaves your organization, a designated staff advocate or the executive director should always ask these few hard questions in an official exit interview, or even in an informal discussion:

- Do you feel you did not fit in culturally?
- Did you have funding issues?
- Were you not able to raise support?
- Did you have a place in this organization, as a person of color, to process events, tragedies, culture, environment, views of new leadership, etc.?
- Did you feel free to give your opinions, even if they might have been different from the status quo?
- Was your voice welcomed at the table in discussions around change?

If it becomes clear the person leaving has experienced some trauma, the organization should be prepared to offer transitional assistance from an outside entity. Mission Training International (www.mti.org) is charged with "equipping and developing cross-cultural messengers of the Gospel." Since 1954, they have worked to prepare missionaries and their families for cross-cultural life and ministry. They can help exiting employees in their transitional process. Another transitional assistance resource is Alongside (www.alongsidecares.net), a counseling retreat ministry for pastors and missionaries who need to be restored and renewed.

Grace compares her early years in urban missions to her current position. Like her former campus ministry team, her organization is dedicated to reconciliation—both external and internal. Organizations seeking structural change must look within and ask tough questions. Is it fair to minorities and women? Can people of color advance in the structure? Are their voices heard? Do organizations have time to reconcile internal wounds when they are battling injustices that affect entire communities or an entire group of marginalized people?

Grace reflects on this:

One of the challenges we are facing is whether focusing inward to deal with the need for reconciliation detracts from directing energies outward. With most organizations, if inward reconciliation detracts, it usually doesn't happen. People grin and bear it and pretend these internal dynamics don't exist. These very white-run organizations never become reconciling communities; however, dealing with the inward questions of reconciliation helps organizations become accountable. Dealing with inward issues will help our mission outwardly. We are in the process of doing that. The staff is mostly white, mostly from the Midwest. Folks are open and want to do good, and they often do; but sometimes there is a rub of culture. When one group dominates, minority opinions often are just that—minority.

Grace knows she's valued but questions whether she is respected or viewed as a leader.

I have been trusted with a lot. Genuine trust is given to me to represent the organization outside. Within the first month of my hiring, they had allowed me to envision and create. But that's one of the burdens of being an African American in a leadership role. It's always having others question your ability. I wonder, is this questioning [rooted in] a lack of respect? Is it a lack of trust? Or is it an issue of authority? These are the questions I'm asking right now and will probably always have to ask being a person of color in authority within a white organization.

Ralph

Missions heroes have challenged racial boundaries and provided great insights. They have suffered yet incredibly have remained faithful and diligent. Ralph, an African American, has made a significant contribution to urban missions through many years of service at a student-led campus ministry. He knows what African Americans in urban missions are up against. He has introduced many students on black college campuses to Jesus and then helped them foster a relationship with the Lord. He also helped students who were away from home for the first time to understand what it means to be a Christian as a young adult, merging into maturity.

Upon exiting college, he felt a commitment to young adults:

As a student, I felt a commitment to God, a calling that I should serve young adults, ages eighteen to twenty-five. But if you want to make more headway in really serving students, you have to address infrastructural issues. I was concerned with making the organization safer for people of color, safer for staff, and safer for students. When I started, I was one of very few black staff in the whole country. Those numbers have changed now. There's a difference in the organization; they have more people of color working in the organization now. Culture changes; nothing is stagnant. But in some ways the culture has stayed the same. I'm African American, yet black people are not monolithic. We must ask: Is there representation of the diversity within the African American community in the organization?

In the early days, Ralph, like many other leaders of color, had to take inventory on how far and quickly he would move up the ladder. Ralph chose to slow his career process and became very familiar with the nuances and values of his organization. He learned how success was defined and how it was rewarded. "I think I became the de facto leader because of tenure, my orientation toward impatience, and my willingness to speak up. What caused me to be a leader is I was willing to take a risk and say some things." Ralph later learned from African American friends that he intimidated white leaders and that things he said were not as "palatable as they preferred."

Toward the end of Ralph's tenure, a position opened and he challenged the leadership to consider why certain people move forward and others do not.

There were two paths to leadership in most missions organizations. First, were you able to raise money? If you raise support, you meet your budget, you get paid, and you're allowed freedom to do your job of ministry. If you don't do these things, you take pay cuts, you take budget cuts and spend more time trying to find funding or working at a lower wage to do your ministry. Consequently, people of color struggled—most often, Latinos or blacks, but some Asians as well and Native Americans—the few on staff. You had to raise money. The economic piece was a good way to get into leadership.

"The other path to leadership was success in terms of numbers reached. These two strengths can offset whatever deficiencies you may have. Because you're strong in raising money, because you're successful in getting students involved, you may have deficiencies that get overlooked or minimized. If you can grow your chapter and sustain it, that's success.

Ralph's insight brings light to an ongoing problem. White missions leaders whose character and methods are questionable at best are often allowed to stay on staff and minister because they raise or connect to money. We turn our heads because they have resources and lose many talented people of color because they do not.

Ralph has had many black people support him, but still recognizes the difficulty.

You send a kid off to college for four years, he graduates with a degree. He gets a job that pays him. Missions work is not well articulated in the black community. It's hard to understand a job that requires the college grad to go find his own salary. If we were articulating that we are pastors on these campuses, the response would be "Oh, I get it; you're building churches over there, or you're building faith communities."

Ralph reflects on a time when he led an urban program.

White people would see our day camp. It was almost like the latest version of the world's fair at the turn of the last century in New York when they used to bring in Pygmies in cages so people could observe these small African people. We felt we were on display. When you have to go to white people to get money so you can minister, there is an underlying, nagging, subconscious reality. It's codependency, mutual exploitation. The white people clear their conscience by doing a good deed. The black kid says, "If you're going to give me some money to work at this day camp, I'll take it." When you put a person of color—someone black, Latino, or Asian—to stand alongside that white person, you disrupt that dynamic and have the greatest impact.

Ralph's words are strong and direct and may result in some discomfort. They are meant to push those of us working in urban missions into community and to challenge the status quo.

Those who are most successful in urban missions sometimes have to be the most bicultural; that is, learn to operate in both worlds. I call such people bridges. They learn to appreciate and highlight the best gifts of different cultures and to work within those differences. Often people who are most successful in the missions world can do that well and over long periods of time.

Monica

I was raised in the South in a caring community. My mother was one of the key people in her community. The community cared for its people; it cared for itself. People had gardens and they shared with others, especially old people.

When I went away to college, I was part of a student ministry organization. It had a mission and was very strategic about who we were reaching out to. At the time I was there—at the beginning—only white students were part of the ministry. I was targeted by a staff person, who did later tell me that. She began to target me because I love people. My dorm room was always packed with people. We just hung out all the time. When she found out I was a Christian, she invited me to some of the ministry's meetings, to Bible study. I enjoyed going. It was nice to be around other Christians. Because of my participation, the organization grew, and by the time I graduated, [the ministry] was 70 percent African American. I was actively recruiting. I felt black people needed to know about this work. The reasons they had not participated before was they didn't know the ministry existed. Seeing me there, seeing that I was "normal" created a safe place for African American students.

Whites would say, "Your ministry is to African American students on campus," and I began to wonder, "What's really happening? You think I can't lead white people?" The ministry leaders had to sit back and think. One of their responses was "We thought you would be more comfortable with the black students or those students would be more comfortable with you." There was an assumption about what was more comfortable for African American leaders, what we can handle. That had to be broken down.

At a retreat that gathered students from different campuses, students from the same college roomed together. Each campus had a few black women; the African American women were all housed in the same rooms, regardless of their college.

"There was this separation!" said Monica, her voice still ringing in disbelief. "It was very clear, and I thought, 'This is crazy!' Of course, I was happy to meet the other black women students and hear their stories, and we had a great time. But I also realized that this was clearly racist."

> I went to the leader on our campus and told her how it looked to me. And she, of course, broke down in tears. She said, "That was not our purpose. We were not trying to segregate. We wanted the African Americans from all the campuses to meet you and the other African American leaders. We wanted them to meet people of color in the organization."

The white leaders had gotten together and decided, "This is what we need to do for them," and didn't invite any African American women into the conversation. A woman of color would have probably said, "This looks bad. This looks like segregation. And that's not going to work." The lack of invitation to the table caused the blow up. White leaders were planning for African American women without our participation. It was not a positive experience.

Monica worked with the college organization for a short time after graduating but desired to be in the urban missions field. While attending a racially mixed church in the South, she heard about a church in a northern city where the pastor was doing great things. When she moved there, she immediately started attending services at the church and volunteered in its after-school program.

Monica eventually became executive director at the nonprofit corporation that had spun off from the community development organization. The founders were two white pastors who had moved into the struggling community and started a church. The white pastor led a staff of color. When the pastor took a leave of absence, no one had been trained to take his place and only he had connections to the funders. Without leadership training, without funders, the situation spiraled out of control. Eventually Monica left. She looks back on hard lessons learned:

When I first got there, they didn't have an executive director, only the white pastor, a director of education, and an assistant pastor, both of whom were African American.

I didn't know there was another person above the pastor who held the power. He had actually started the organization in another city. He remained faceless, but he definitely was the guy making the pieces move. After I had been there only a couple of months, the founder met with me and said, "We want to make you the executive director of the corporation." That was going to make me my supervisor's supervisor. I was shocked. I was very young, part-time, and still new to the organization.

Monica assumed the role of executive director, immediately becoming supervisor to the director of education, another black woman.

Assuming leadership was awkward, at times difficult. I started reading about what it meant to fund and to lead an organization. In the beginning, I asked if I could take some classes and the response was "Oh, you don't need any classes. Ask us. We'll tell you." But when you don't know the questions to ask, you can't ask them.

When the pastor left on sabbatical, I was given complete control over everything—all the bank accounts, everything. Basically, I was running the church and the organization. It was kind of crazy. At times, when we were both away, he would say, "This makes me nervous that neither one of us is there."

As I read more, I saw we were supposed to have a real board over this organization that held regular meetings. On paper, there was a board of directors, but I didn't know who was on the board, and I was the executive director! We didn't have regular meetings. Before things turned sour—which makes me sad—it was very much like a family.

But there also was a power dynamic—a struggle that always existed with money. The pastor handled all of the fund-raising.

He was gifted in that area. He held the funders close to him. He would say, "These are *my* funders." He raised the money through the church and then wrote a check to the corporation. I had to go to him all the time saying, "We need more money. We need more money!"

Although the pastor was white, there were many Asian funders because the church that he came from was a very powerful international church. The pastor had contacts with Asians within the congregation who gave [large sums] on a regular basis. The funding mostly came from Christian people who were Asian or white men.

That list of funders disturbed me. I look at ministry as sharing the Gospel, but also as taking care of self. I began to push to become self-sufficient instead of depending on these outside funders. I expressed that we needed to bring in funders who supported the organization and were not just supporting him.

There were meetings to which I was not invited. Decisions were brought to me and presented as if I was part of the decision-making process. The church's pastoral council was treated the same way. I was supposed to encourage the pastoral council to do what the two white founders wanted.

Evangelical whites wanted to be a part of "the movement." African Americans have a story of survival. We're not perfect, but we've survived. It's a pretty powerful story that doesn't get told or celebrated often enough. With white leaders, blacks get a sense of being taken care of. For example, a lady was a single mom, a very strong woman. The church, led by a white pastor, saw her as a woman with a lot of children and offered, "If you need some help, we'll pay your light bill." She began to give them her light bill saying, "My light bill is due. I'm behind in my electric bill."

She became dependent. We were handicapping people instead of helping them. I found that quite disturbing and brought it up. It wasn't received too well. White leadership becomes "We'll take care of you. We will go get the money and you don't have to give." That is a disservice and unbiblical.

I didn't want to be part of a system that was damaging to our community and to me. I left for my own health. I was vocal about what I didn't think was proper, even about spending and how the money was being used. I would come home in tears because of what was happening. There were racial overtones as to why I left. Whites put you in power, but you are not really in power. Every African American—old and young—who left felt the same way. I told the pastor, "Every person who has left has left broken. I'm trying to leave here whole." When the pastor left, all of the funders stopped giving.

White people give money to white people, but leaders of color shouldn't lose their sense of self because of that. Trust your leadership qualities. I looked to someone else—to whites—to validate me, but my leadership and ability to work with people were gifts from God. We look to white people for the answers instead of God. Whatever the white pastor says goes. That's what happened at this church.

Whites wanting to serve in an urban setting need to do research. Ask questions. Pray. Ask, why did you decide to do this? Why this community? Why inner-city missions? Why black people? Why did you decide to make this move? Why not poor white people? There are more of them than [poor blacks].

Be aware of those who may have good intentions but with a "savior mentality." The white pastor left us hanging without support because he lived in a romantic world, trying to build on a broken foundation. That happens quite often. Missionaries get tired; after a while it's not romantic anymore and they leave.

The nonprofit survived and continues to do work.

Monica's example reminds us to ask the right questions before we move into ministry, questions that will determine who we work with and how we work with others, and that will help us unpack our deeper motives.

The call of God is a powerful voice within our being. When we are called, a force is driving us. When we are not careful, we can put ourselves or power dynamics at the center of our work and lose sight of God's call. If we do this, we'll end up easily walking away.

In most missions organizations, you're going to get tired, frustrated, and not have the funding you want. When those things happen, the driving force needs to be your calling, mission, people, and justice.

CHAPTER 11

Harmony

"Anything that decolonizes urban ministries is going to be important."

—*Anton Flores*

T here is a beautiful sound that occurs in our lives when who God has made us finds its way into our everyday existence. Wrestling through the tough questions about missions that people of color bring to the table grows missions. Sweeping these issues under the carpet and avoiding the conversations prevent creative solutions and shut the door to the kingdom. Most of us—red, yellow, brown, black, or white—long for healing, and yet at the same time, we are afraid to pursue it. Theologian Howard Thurman expresses these feelings best in his commencement address at Spelman College, which has become the much-quoted "Sound of the Genuine."

There is something in every one of you that waits, listens for the sound of the genuine in yourself and if you cannot hear it, you will never find whatever it is for which you are searching and if you hear it and then do not follow it, it was better that you had never been born...

You are the only you that has ever lived; your idiom is the only idiom of its kind in all of existence and if you cannot hear the sound of the genuine in you, you will all of your life spend your days on the ends of strings that somebody else pulls...

There is in you something that waits and listens for the sound of the genuine in yourself and sometimes there is so much traffic going on in your minds, so many different kinds of signals, so many vast impulses floating through your organism that go back thousands of generations, long before you were even a thought in the mind of creation, and you are buffeted by these, and in the midst of all of this you have got to find out what your name is. Who are you? How does the sound of the genuine come through to you...

The sound of the genuine is flowing through you. Don't be deceived and thrown off by all the noises that are a part even of your dreams, your ambitions, so that you don't hear the sound of the genuine in you, because that is the only true guide that you will ever have, and if you don't have that you don't have a thing. You may be famous, you may be whatever the other ideals are which are a part of this generation but you know you don't have the foggiest notion of who you are, where you are going, what you want. Cultivate the discipline of listening to the sound of the genuine in yourself.

Now there is something in everybody that waits and listens for the sound of the genuine in other people. And it is so easy to say that anybody who looks like him or her, anybody who acts as this person acts, can't hear any sound of the genuine. I must wait and listen for the sound of the genuine in you. I must wait.

For if I cannot hear it, then in my scheme of things, you are not even present. And everybody wants to feel that everybody else knows that she is there.

I have a blind friend who just became blind after she was a grown woman. I asked her: "What is the greatest disaster that your blindness has brought to you?" She said, "When I go places where there are people, I have a feeling that nobody knows that I'm here. I can't see any recognition, I can't see... and if nobody knows that I'm here, it's hard for me to know where I am."

There is something that waits and listens for the sound of the genuine in your mother, in your father, in the people you can't stand, and if you had the power you would wipe them out. But instinctively you know that if you wipe them out, you go with them. So you fight for your own life by finding some way to get along with them without killing them. There is something in you that waits and listens for the sound of the genuine in other people. And if you can't hear it, then you are reduced by that much.

If I were to ask you what is the thing that you desire most in life this afternoon, you would say a lot of things off the top of your head, most of which you wouldn't believe but you would think that you were saying the things that I thought you ought to think that you should say. But I think that if you were stripped to whatever there is in you that is literal and irreducible, and you tried to answer that question, the answer may be something like this: I want to feel that I am thoroughly and completely understood so that now and then I can take my guard down and look out around me and not feel that I will be destroyed with my defenses down. I want to feel completely vulnerable, completely naked, completely exposed and absolutely secure.

This is what you look for in your children when you have them, this is what you look for in your husband if you get one. That I can run the risk of radical exposure and know that the eye that beholds my vulnerability will not step on me. That I can feel secure in my awareness of the active presence of my own idiom in me. So as I live my life then, this is what I am trying to fulfill. It doesn't matter whether I become a doctor, lawyer, housewife. I'm secure because I hear the sound of the genuine in myself and having learned to listen to that, I can become quiet enough, still enough, to hear the sound of the genuine in you.

Now if I hear the sound of the genuine in me, and if you hear the sound of the genuine in you, it is possible for me to go down in me and come up in you. So that when I look at myself through your eyes having made that pilgrimage, I see in me what you see in me and the wall that separates and divides will disappear and we will become one because the sound of the genuine makes the same music.

Life's Assignment

Now this is your assignment and you can never say again that nobody told you.

Go thy way,

All things say

Thou hast thy way to go

Thou hast thy day to live

Thou hast thy need of thee to make in the hearts of others.

Do thy thing and be thou sure of this:

No other can do for thee that appointed thee of God

Not any light shall fall upon thy road for other eyes

Thee the angel calls as he calls others

And thy life to thee is precious as the greatest life can be to Him

So live thy life and go thy way

So that God will not have to forgive Himself for letting you be born.

There is in every person that which waits, waits, waits and listens for the sound of the genuine in herself. There is that in every person that waits—waits and listens—for the sound of the genuine in other people. And when these two sounds come together, this is the music God heard when He said, "Let us make man in our image."

Howard Thurman's speech is a reminder that each of us was formed uniquely in God's image to give our individual gifts to the world. What people of color uniquely offer has slowly been negated or dismissed in the name of missions. The genuineness of who we are as African descended, Latino, Asian, or Native American has been silenced. Many who would speak out are quiet for fear of losing an opportunity or retaliation by someone in power. We often sit silent as our culture and dignity washes away each day.

To those silent ones, I urge you to listen to your own sound. You are fearfully and wonderfully made. Listen to the sound. You have nothing to fear. Listen to the sound. God loves you. Your voice is beautiful. Listen to your sound. You can lead. Your family has to eat. You need a place to live. You need school for your children. Listen to the sound. It will provide for you, bring life to your bones and hope to your being.

If we never let our genuine voice be heard, we will never be free. I am not the first nor will I be the last to say freedom costs. Do we want someone else constantly defining who we are and dictating how we should proceed? Should any other human being denigrate the unique way we know, love, approach, and worship God? The call to serve is for everyone and should not be dictated by one culture nor have leadership dominated by one group.

Let the light of Christ bring peace and harmony to your soul by allowing you to know yourself.

May the hope of the world be known as we know ourselves and show the world the fullness of God as expressed through people of color. We are a part of the beauty of the kingdom. We are not a mistake, not a sidebar, and not voices to be restricted. We can only reflect that unique beauty of God as we get in touch with the genuine inside ourselves.

I pray you will know yourself as God sees you, and when you see the genuine you, that you feel no shame and give thanks to the one who created us all.

CHAPTER 12

How Dare You! White Response to New *Missio Dei*

"Helping doesn't mean you need to lead. Sometimes you need to follow. Following is a good way to learn something new."

—*Dennis*

Idioms like "Pull yourself up by your own bootstraps" and "God bless the child that has its own" are terms I understand, but they have become the mantra of the middle class. This value system says it is not acceptable to need something—to have to ask someone for something or to be the object of someone's service. The middle class tends to be more comfortable playing the hero role and all that comes with it.

It makes us feel better about ourselves when we serve someone, but the middle class must realize that the people being served also have something to offer that can enhance their lives in turn. Part of our service is to authentically listen to people we serve in an effort to learn and share friendship. This calls for middle-class folks to acknowledge their own need and then be willing to allow someone from among the so-called needy to meet it.

Mutual service is hard for middle-class people. They don't like to be served. They like to serve.

Glenn Balzer, executive director of DOOR, whom we met in chapter 3, "Diversity at Work in the *Missio Dei*," has experienced the dissent of white missions volunteers when efforts are made to put the new perspectives into practice in urban missions.

Dennis, an affable young African American urbanite, was one of Glenn's former staff members.

> Dennis spent over a decade with DOOR. He was in junior high school when I first met him. The church that hosted our Chicago program was his home church. He was fascinated by all the white kids who wanted to come to East Garfield Park and serve. He was famous for teaching groups to play Ultimate Frisbee in the hood. It was a privilege to watch him grow. He went to college on scholarship but came back every summer to work at DOOR. After graduating with a degree in communications, we hired him full-time as the assistant director, and within two years he was the Chicago city director.

While Glenn applauded and promoted Dennis, the adult missions volunteers who felt their experience with DOOR could have been better expressed the kinds of evaluations leaders of color often receive from whites in summer missions program. Some of their comments are included here.

"Capable is not the best choice of word in my opinion for Dennis." (Summer Volunteer #1)

"I felt like they could have been more knowledgeable and more mature. Sometimes I felt like I had another youth with me instead of a leader." (Summer Volunteer #2)

After reading the evaluations, Glenn responded: "Initially, I accepted the 'inexperienced' comments at face value. Over time it has become clear that the 'inexperienced' label is overwhelmingly directed to our staff of color."

Glenn continues, "This following evaluation is interesting: Jane is a white mother and 'they' are a Hispanic male and the other support staff of color."

"Jane was an exception, and without her it felt like they were either going through the motions, or were enthusiastic but not all that sure of what they were to be doing." (Summer Volunteer #3)

"Was it immaturity or just a different worldview? Again, at first I took this at face value, but the immature comments always seem to be directed at the staff of color."

"I found that navigating DOOR staff's capacity to offer supervision for our youth challenging and confusing... It was stressful for me because I didn't trust the staff's maturity or ability to make good decisions." (Summer Volunteer #4)

To the feedback below, Glenn comments, "I suspect that the communication skills have much more to do with his accent."

"[The Hispanic staff member] tried and was gracious, but he lacked some of the organizational skills that a group of our size requires. His communication skills were not ideal, and oftentimes it felt like we had to tell him how to do his job." (Summer Volunteer #5)

In this evaluation, the women were white, and the male a person of color:

"The three women who helped were great, really enjoyed them. The one guy who helped, and I don't even remember his name was not good at all. The week we arrived was just after his high school graduation. Staff like that are too young. In some cases they are attempting to lead their peers and that just doesn't work." (Summer Volunteer #6)

The criticisms are all based on the missions volunteers needing to be served, shown, and otherwise have their own expectations met for personal guidance, security, and cultural comfort. Perhaps the black and Hispanic male leaders were not too young, immature, or ill prepared to serve the community where the missions work was directed, but rather, simply did not cater to the missions volunteers and white savior syndrome attitudes?

Dennis, twenty-seven years old and six feet two inches tall, is described by others as having a strong presence, but he reveals parts of his personality that belie his public, controlled stance. "I'm an introvert," he says. "And I love to read. I enjoy reading comics and watching movies with my wife!"

Dennis had been involved in youth missions programs and

after-school missions since he was five years old via his church, which was very active in missions and community development. He served with DOOR based on his pastor's recommendation. By the time he came to DOOR as a junior in high school, he had years of leadership experience working with other youth and on short-term summer missions.

Being part of DOOR was a big thing for me growing up as a kid. I met a lot of different people from all over the country, even Canada. They were people whom I probably would never have had a conversation with if it had not been for the program. But you find out you have a lot in common. Some people I still stay in contact with on Facebook.

As I became an adult, I realized the impact the program had on the community, both positive and negative. The positive list could go on and on. I saw people who actually cared and wanted to understand, even if they didn't understand the problems of the inner city. The fact that they came showed that they wanted to participate in some way. I saw them give not only their time and their energy, but also their money. That's how much that organization meant to them.

The negative is that people from other communities come in thinking they are showing they can do things better than you. That's just one stigma. It wasn't culture shock for me to participate in the program. I was used to all kinds of people, as my church is multicultural.

It was harder for me when I became an assistant director. One person thought I couldn't teach her group anything. I never understood that. She didn't think the program lived up to what it was advertising. She said it was my fault, because I didn't have the experience needed. For example, if I wasn't a pastor, she felt I couldn't teach scripture. But I had held this kind of job for ten years!

The kids were very eager and open to a new experience. The adults were really closed, and I don't really understand why. I had a lot of frustration. You try so hard to do a good job but the person complains.

For example, on the way to a site, our group would be harassed by the police officers. This is East Garfield Park, one of the poorest communities in Chicago. You have a group of white kids walking with an African American male down the street and the police officer asks them, "Are you in trouble? Do you need assistance? Is he trying to sell you drugs?" Bluntly, the police would tell them that they shouldn't be in that community. He's an officer of the peace. I'm doing missions work, yet the police looked at me as a threat! How do you explain that to someone who doesn't know what that's about? This is my community. How do I explain that this is the way the police officer greets me?

We had a Bible camp on the north side of the city. There was a shooting two blocks away. Nobody was hurt. But how do you sit down and have a discussion about seeing the face of God in that incident? These are real-world situations that happen, not on a daily basis, but they happen. How do you explain that to these groups? The young people were anxious to help. A lot of them were scared. No one was ever hurt in the program while I was there.

What helped me through the crisis was to see others of color in the program. I knew I couldn't be the only person who could do this work. Sometimes you have to step aside for others.

Dennis left DOOR after ten years. "I have no regrets. It was a life choice. I got married and I got burnt out. It takes a lot of energy and a lot of spirit to do that type of program for so long. The burnout was mostly from my own self-reflection. I asked myself, 'Am I making a difference for or am I mascot for the participants? Am I a social experiment, or am I more than that?' "

Glenn recounts a statement Dennis made during his exit interview that especially stuck out. "I am tired of having to be the representative of all black males."

"There was a group that still comes to the program," muses Dennis.

They are from Iowa. They come every spring for a weekend. In that group, I met an African American man who lives in a white community. I got attached to him immediately as his experience was similar to mine. My church is 90 percent Anglo, 10 percent African American, Hispanic, and South African. We both had a multicultural background, and most African Americans can't say that because they are so closed off. Not because of anything they've done, but because of what society has done to them. I was blessed to have that experience, and to see someone else with that background for me was quite joyous.

Dennis offers this advice to people of color who want to work in urban missions: "Be willing to be challenged, not just physically, but emotionally. It's really character building."

For whites coming in from outside the city, he says, "Be open.

Helping doesn't mean you need to lead. Sometimes you need to follow. Following is a good way to learn something new."

Advice for whites who want to work in urban missions

John Tramel, a great friend and white brother I have had the privilege of getting to know and work with over the years, shared his perspective.

> It is vital for white people who are committed to racial and economic justice to seek out leadership, accountability, and feedback from people of color. The dominant narrative of our culture has continuously glorified the realities and offerings of white people, while at the same time minimizing and denying the realities and offerings of people of color. This creates a blinding privilege that prevents white people from being able to fully see and understand the best path toward justice, and makes it inevitable that we will reinforce and collude with the dominant narrative when operating outside true relationships with people of color.
>
> To overcome the inevitability of unintentionally reinforcing race and class stereotypes and inequality, we (white folks) must seek out authentic cross-cultural relationships where we listen and learn from the experiences and wisdom of brothers and sisters of color, who live with, on a daily basis, the misrepresentation of the dominant narrative. Through these relationships, we must be willing to not only address racism in society, but we also must be

willing to hear feedback about how it is manifested in our own attitudes, beliefs, and behaviors.

We must immerse ourselves continuously with the cultural and artistic expressions and testimonies of people of color that can pull back the scales of blindness from our eyes grown by years of submersion in white privilege. White people must do these things with complete open minds and hearts free from the historic defensiveness and guilt that only protects the status quo and prevents our ongoing transformation. As Lilla Watson, indigenous Australian artist, academic, and activist, said, "If you have come here to help, then you are wasting our time. But if you have come because your liberation is bound up with mine, then let us work together."

It's often difficult for whites to respect black leadership, particularly young African American leaders. While Glenn has seen changes at the top at DOOR—a board that is primarily people of color—the laypeople, usually adults who participate in the weeklong camps with their church youth, still find it a challenge to take direction from those not like them. Following a person young enough to be your child is difficult for those of any race or ethnicity. Taking orders from someone from the inner city—someone whom they doubt has the wisdom or worldly knowledge to teach privileged kids anything of value—requires a mental reset. But if urban missions are to be led by leaders from the inside of the communities served, those venturing in for short-term service must change their mind-set.

I understand that this might be a difficult process and that the decisions white leaders have to make are decisions for their own call, livelihoods, and professional careers, as they see it. In the larger scheme of justice, globally most of the people being "served" are people of color. Our missions work has lacked the diversity necessary for it to be as effective as it could be. There is a dearth of leaders of color, voices of people who are living in communities that are being "served." The intentions for most are rooted in a strong sense of call, but we have to correct this void.

Perhaps there's a sense that people are not grateful for the generosity being shown to them. Many whites, even those actively engaged in missions, wrestle with the belief that people of color are less civilized and inferior. They are perceived as unable to lead or to set up systems on their own without white leadership. These notions go completely against the teachings of scripture. If God has created us in God's image, such notions have to be lies. What have we done as human beings to corrupt the world that God created for all of us to enjoy? My call is for us to work to bring that world into existence.

Whites sensing a call to urban missions should learn the perspectives of people of color. Read their books, be in genuine relationships with them, watch their films and TV shows, attend their church services, and make such exposure an ongoing, regular, and forever part of your lifestyle. Go to the movies on the other side of town. Grow your perspective. Let this learning influence your thinking.

Invest in a small grassroots organization somewhere in the world without personally taking a leadership role. And if you do get involved, resist the temptation to direct anything during your first year of involvement.

If you are leading a 501(c)(3) ministry or missions organization, invest in a person of color to step into senior leadership within your organization. Put them in a position to be considered for your role, if and when it becomes open.

If you find yourself in a place where a person of color is leading you, know and be prepared for their leadership to be culturally different and uncomfortable for you. (Just as it is difficult for people of color to be in a monocultural environment.)

In many communities of color, perfectionism is not honored as a virtue. Excellence—doing something well—and hard work are valued, but perfectionism is a weight on the soul that insists that you're always presented in a way that seems like you have everything together, even if you don't. Perfectionism and excellence are not the same. Excellence is that the mission was accomplished. Perfectionism is the appearance of flawlessness in every aspect. Most of the time circumstances are not flawless, and we are left with a less than real existence, one that is not authentic, open, honest, or human. When one does not have a cultural need to appear perfect, it leads to a judgment regarding excellence. A white leader might believe a leader of color is not concerned about doing things right, when they are making a judgment based on perfectionism. Perfectionism can't distinguish between the times when excellence is needed and when it's okay to relax.

White response to new *Missio Dei*—I'll follow you!

Be okay with following. As a white person, you don't have to have control. You can enjoy following. Know that God cares for you and that people of color care for you. They are good people who have a different perspective, but they genuinely care for you. There are many people of color who are not angry, who understand and love all people, and who can understand and love you.

Shawn Casselberry, executive director of Mission Year, shared his two very different experiences with urban missions leadership, which have led him to a view of "mutual submission":

> I was part of a multiracial church plant that went horribly wrong. The majority white church I attended "partnered" with a majority African American church in our college town to plant a multiracial church in a nearby city.
>
> It looked great on paper: a white pastor and a black pastor coming together from two segregated congregations to give witness to the reconciling power of the Gospel. (And it looked great on the billboard the church paid for, too!)
>
> I was drawn to this vision from my own experience growing up in segregated neighborhoods and churches and always having a gnawing feeling that this division was counter to what God intended for us.
>
> I longed for relationship and community with my African American brothers and sisters and thought, "What better way to tear down the barriers than to worship together and start a new kind of church?"
>
> So I put my energy into this effort until it slowly crashed and burned. We were all scratching our heads wondering what the heck happened? How could God let such a worthy cause derail?
>
> What derailed this effort is the same thing that derails so many genuine attempts at reconciliation. Power. There was a power imbalance.

Everyone on the leadership team of the church plant, except the black pastor, was from the white church. The white church provided the majority of the money, so the white church felt like it had the authority to call the shots. The black pastor preached on alternating Sundays, but the day-to-day decisions of the church were controlled and made by the white pastor and congregation.

Pretty soon the black pastor stopped coming to the leadership meetings out of frustration while the white church saw this lack of involvement as further proof that he was not really committed.

The church lasted only a year and a half until it crumbled.

When I relocated to Chicago I had this experience fresh in my mind. I decided going to a multiracial church was not enough. I needed to plant myself in an African American community, not from a position of power, but of submission.

I made up my mind to submit my white instincts to lead, control, fix, and dominate. I felt like a character in *The Lord of the Rings* trying to avoid the lure of the ring of power that so easily distorts and destroys lives (and ministries). I decided I would not seek to lead in the community, but to place myself under local African American leaders. I wouldn't try to start my own organization or church, but support the dreams and visions of the community. I wouldn't seek my own advantage, but leverage my privilege and resources for the community's benefit.

Soong-Chan Rah, a professor at North Park University, is a prophetic voice for the church in the area of racism and multiethnicity. At a roundtable discussion on race, he was asked what white people can do to address the power dynamic that so often befalls reconciliation. He suggested white people place themselves underneath people of color. He said they should seek a mentor from whom they can learn. When white people put themselves in the place of learner, they challenge the power imbalance. He says the majority of people of color have had to submit to white leaders, be it pastors, teachers, professors, or bosses. The majority of white people have not had to submit to leaders of color. By choosing to do so, they open doors for amazing opportunities for partnership and growth.

This is something we feel strongly about at Mission Year, so we intentionally partner with churches and organizations where our team members can serve underneath community leaders of color. This allows our white team members to practice submission so they can enjoy meaningful cross-cultural relationships.

It is also empowering for team members of color to see strong, respected, diverse leaders who are passionately pursuing God's call. And lastly, it is incredibly affirming for the leaders themselves. Sadly, too many leaders of color have experienced the discouragement and paternalism of well-intentioned white people who do not know how to practice mutual submission.

For the last nine years I have experienced the joy that comes from living among, working under, and being mentored by tremendously gifted leaders of color. As I have done this, I have been able to build authentic relationships based on trust and mutual respect. I have also been able to grow by listening and learning from those who are doing kingdom work in the community.

I will always seek out ways to overturn the power imbalance until we have true mutuality in missions and in the church. I believe this is vital to the work of the Gospel.

The prophet Isaiah said the work of the Messiah would include hills being brought low and valleys being raised. This is the movement of the Gospel. Those with privilege are humbled through voluntary submission and service, while those that have been disadvantaged are raised through empowerment and leadership.

This mutual movement creates equality, which allows us to meet as equals and friends. When this equality is achieved, together we will experience the glory of the Lord.

Every valley shall be raised up, every mountain and hill made low, the rough ground shall become level, the rugged places a plain. And the glory of the Lord will be revealed, and all people will see it together. For the mouth of the Lord has spoken.
—Isaiah 40:4–5, NIV

I know many whites who make their homes in communities of color. They choose to be part of communities of color because diversity brings them joy and life. They have found friendship, caring neighbors, and genuine admiration for the cultures among which they live. They often interact with other whites—sometimes in their own families—who have the "How dare you?" response. They lament and are saddened by such responses and use such interactions as teaching moments. They also go out of their way to encourage leaders of color when they face racist responses.

Diversity has an element of God's presence that allows us to see past ourselves, to not get our own way, but to be satisfied to be part of something significant.

CHAPTER 13

Who Will Lead the Way?

"I'm not saying that things are great here. I'm not saying that people don't have cultural blind spots, make inappropriate jokes or statements, and even sometimes act questionably. But in terms of their genuineness toward me I can say that it's been real. It's been great."

—*Andre*

Andre is young, African American, and a senior director of mobilization and candidacy in a predominantly white missions organization. He fits well within the culture and is being groomed for higher leadership. He has a budget, travels, and represents the organization. By all accounts he does a "good job" but experiences seasons of loneliness as the only person of color on a staff of twenty-five. He also misses opportunities for mentorship by African Americans in missions.

Andre had a full scholarship to a historically black college and planned to be a scientist. Then, as he puts it, he "fell in love with Jesus" and wanted to be an evangelist. He transferred to Oral Roberts University. "I love my Afrocentric sisters and brothers, but it is not the core of who I am. There's something deeper than that. That was something I was hoping to find at ORU, and I think I did find it." In 1998, a short-term trip to Uganda was his first exposure to cross-cultural mission work. About five years later, he was named the missions director at an African American megachurch, but found it wasn't a good fit and began to look elsewhere.

> Someone from the missions organization was looking to move to another role in the organization, and he wanted me to be his replacement. So he contacted me specifically for that purpose, and I ended up getting the job. We would do a lot of other things, but my job was specifically cross-cultural, oversees.
>
> As a leader, I tend to be insecure in my decision making. I might not be as aggressive in pursuing things that we should do. I might be a little more repressed emotionally. In an African American context, I might be a little more alive in terms of energy and silliness. I've been given adequate authority. I have great freedom in terms of my budget. I'm respected. If there is a decision that needs to be made that affects my department, even my superior will say, 'I didn't want to make this decision because that's your role, not mine.' They defer to my authority.

The organization has a typical structure: a president, board of directors, a layer of senior directors and directors. Andre has moved up rather quickly and another promotion is on the horizon.

> Do I see myself moving up in the organization? Yes, and the organization has communicated that to me, both our previous president and our current president. We have the president's gathering where we invite major donors to learn about our

ministry. It takes place in Florida. The president wants me to go to those gatherings. He wants me to learn how to interface with donors. My boss is always investing in me. He wants me to go into the mission field. Everyone indicates that if I stay here long enough, I will become a vice president. It hasn't been stated verbally, but that's the path I'm being taken on.

When I started here, we had five African Americans on staff. Through a series of moving or layoffs, I'm the only one left. One lady was very expressive in her faith. When we had morning devotions, she would sometimes shout or dance or take a lap around the building. If I wanted to do that, I wouldn't. I would be too embarrassed or afraid of being perceived a certain way or fitting into a stereotype. Sometimes I wonder how much of the real me is working in this job. And what I would be if there were more diversity on the staff.

I have the same experience as I serve on another board. I wonder what I would be like if most of the people on the board weren't older white guys. I don't want to be perceived as a Malcolm X or a Black Panther, so I hold back. I tend to be less sure of myself. I spend a lot of time wondering. When I'm in a meeting, I want to say, share my thoughts, but I'm thinking, "How do I sound? Am I pronouncing my words correctly? Are my hands in the right place? Is my attitude good?" I spend so much time thinking about things that have nothing to do with the pure meeting topics. Adjusting is always taking place.

The presidential election had just taken place. That was uncomfortable, very uncomfortable for me. I don't want to tell people what I think because I'm afraid they will label me an ignorant guy who's voting for a black guy because I'm black. I feel a disconnect. But the people here have invested so much in me relationally. We've done things together so that I'm able to work through some of those hurdles, and it still does feel a little awkward.

I grew up in a thriving middle class of people who were engineers, doctors, and lawyers. You know, good people. When they told someone in the organization that I grew up in a predominantly black community, in their minds they saw the projects, the ghetto, and I was one who escaped. I had to adjust. There were no adjustments made for me, as it relates to music, to culture, to other things. But I had a very positive experience.

Andre relates his experience while a student attending a white church.

"Church buses brought black kids from the projects to service, but they weren't seated with the other children. They were bribed into being good, with comments like, 'If you sit down, I'll give you a piece of candy!'" Andre felt the church did not understand how to work with children of color. While he appreciated the church's effort, he was left with the impression that the church didn't view the black children the same as white children.

The strength of his current organization is its ability to contextualize.

We go in with the posture of a learner, of humility. In Lexington, Kentucky, which is predominantly white, the black people there say, "These folks have street credibility. They show up in court when I have court cases, they love me, they invite me into their homes for breakfast and dinner." I think our folks have a lot of credibility in the way they do outreach.

Some whites minister to blacks and assume they can make a single decision and have enough willpower to just lift themselves from their situation. They are oblivious to the systemic issues.

"The onlies"

Andre is an "African American only." Being an "only" comes with a high level of expectation from others.

> I am literally the only African American in the entire country who directs a department of mobilization in a missions agency. Most of the African Americans involved in missions are older than me. I have a good relationship with them and the previous generation. Some look at me as, this is the guy who's going to help us deal with this pressing issue. That's a lot of pressure.
>
> When I was asked to take this job, a very good African American leader I know said to me, "Andre, that organization is interested in hiring you because they want to get their foot in the African American community. And once they do that they are going to fire you." I wondered if he was right, if I was being set up. In my very first interview with the guy who is now our president, my unasked question was answered. He said, "Andre, I want to be very clear. We are not hiring you because we need a token black person on staff. We are hiring you because we believe in you and your skills, and we want you to be a part of our team." And that's the reception I've had ever since.
>
> I'm not saying that things are great here. I'm not saying that people don't have cultural blind spots, make inappropriate jokes

or statements, and even sometimes act questionably. But in terms of their genuineness toward me I can say that it's been real. It's been great.

Our future is bright when it comes to leaders of color. We have young leaders of color who understand a multicultural world. They are unafraid to engage different cultural values, willing to dialogue, and are open to global responsibilities. At the same time, many of them come from families that have struggled with or been touched by poverty personally. This gives them deeper perspective on life and a broader array of experiences. We need to make sure that they understand and connect to history, whether that's the history of the black church, the eradication of the Native American way of life, the journey of Latinos in our country as it relates to immigration, or the perceived invisibility of our Asian brothers and sisters. We need to make sure our young leaders understand these stories.

There is also openness on the part of young white leaders to work in conjunction with leaders of color. That brings hope of a new world, hope of justice.

CHAPTER 14

Hurt but Hopeful

"Our generation goes to conferences like the Justice Conferences or Urbana, and we so easily point out everything that's wrong. 'Where's the power coming from?' we ask. We're trained to see that as something we need to talk about. When I try to take the conversation deeper, it falls apart.

"I was having a conversation with a friend of mine, a white man, older than me, at the Justice Conference. We were talking about what it was like to live in a neighborhood in Atlanta where he is one of the only white people. He was talking about the language, how hard it was to communicate, but he said, 'It's not a race thing.'

"It's always a race thing. Can we take this conversation up another step, to where it actually matters or it is just going to be a bunch of talk? Can our generation talk about the fact that funding isn't coming for people of color and that white people must be willing to actually give up the power?"

—*Jenny Ouseph*

To hope after we are hurt is a powerful tool of healing and offers strength for the rest of the journey. The natural reaction to being hurt by missions is self-protection—withdrawing from missions work. Cynicism and separation have been tried and proven lacking. Hope is a better way. Hope has been tried and proven worthy.

Dr. Martin Luther King Jr.'s "Letter from Birmingham Jail" is one of his most powerful writings. It is still relevant to us today as we reflect on the hurt inflicted by Christian missions. It captures both our hurt and future hope as missionaries and servants of Jesus.

The public statement directed to King by eight Alabama clergymen, which prompted his famous letter, is also instructive as it paints the backdrop for Dr. King's missive.

Eight Alabama Clergymen

4/12/1963

We the undersigned clergymen are among those who, in January, issued "an appeal for law and order and common sense," in dealing with racial problems in Alabama. We expressed understanding that honest convictions in racial matters could properly be pursued in the courts, but urged that decisions of those courts should in the meantime be peacefully obeyed.

Since that time there had been some evidence of increased forbearance and a willingness to face facts. Responsible citizens have undertaken to work on various problems which cause racial friction and unrest. In Birmingham, recent public events have given indication that we all have opportunity for a new constructive and realistic approach to racial problems.

However, we are now confronted by a series of demonstrations by some of our Negro citizens, directed and led in part by outsiders. We recognize the natural impatience of people who feel that their hopes are slow in being realized. But we are convinced that these demonstrations are unwise and untimely.

We agree rather with certain local Negro leadership which has called for honest and open negotiation of racial issues in our area. And we believe this kind of facing of issues can best be accomplished by citizens of our own metropolitan area, white and Negro, meeting with their knowledge and experience of the local situation. All of us need to face that responsibility and find proper channels for its accomplishment.

Just as we formerly pointed out that "hatred and violence have no sanction in our religious and political traditions," we also point out that such actions as incite to hatred and violence, however technically peaceful those actions may be, have not contributed to the resolution of our local problems. We do not believe that these days of new hope are days when extreme measures are justified in Birmingham.

We commend the community as a whole, and the local news media and law enforcement officials in particular, on the calm manner in which these demonstrations have been handled. We urge the public to continue to show restraint should the demonstrations continue, and the law enforcement officials to remain calm and continue to protect our city from violence.

We further strongly urge our own Negro community to withdraw support from these demonstrations, and to unite locally in working peacefully for a better Birmingham. When rights are consistently denied, a cause should be pressed in the courts and in negotiations among local leaders, and not in the streets. We appeal to both our white and Negro citizenry to observe the principles of law and order and common sense.

Bishop C.C.J. Carpenter, D.D., LL.D., Episcopalian Bishop of Alabama

Bishop Joseph A. Durick, D.D., Auxiliary Bishop, Roman Catholic Diocese of Mobile, Birmingham

Rabbi Milton L. Grafman, Temple Emanu-El, Birmingham, Alabama

Bishop Paul Hardin, Methodist Bishop of the Alabama-West Florida Conference

Bishop Nolan B. Harmon, Bishop of the North Alabama Conference of the Methodist Church

Rev. George M. Murray, D.D., LL.D, Bishop Coadjutor, Episcopal Diocese of Alabama

Rev. Edward V. Ramage, Moderator, Synod of the Alabama Presbyterian Church in the United States

Rev. Earl Stallings, Pastor, First Baptist Church, Birmingham, Alabama

April 12, 1963

"Letter from Birmingham Jail"

April 16, 1963

MY DEAR FELLOW CLERGYMEN:

While confined here in the Birmingham City Jail, I came across your recent statement calling my present activities "unwise and untimely." Seldom do I pause to answer criticism of my work and ideas. If I sought to answer all the criticisms that cross my desk, my secretaries would have little time for anything other than such correspondence in the course of the day, and I would have no time for constructive work. But since I feel that you are men of genuine goodwill and that your criticisms are sincerely set forth, I want to try to answer your statements in what I hope will be patient and reasonable terms.

I think I should indicate why I am here in Birmingham, since you have been influenced by the view which argues against "outsiders coming in." I have the honor of serving as president of the Southern Christian Leadership Conference, an organization operating in every Southern state, with headquarters in Atlanta, Georgia. We have some eighty-five affiliated organizations across the South, and one of them is the Alabama Christian Movement for Human Rights. Frequently we share staff, educational and financial resources with our affiliates. Several months ago the affiliate here in Birmingham asked us to be on call to engage in a nonviolent

Enslaving and Christianizing the African

Ironically, it was outrage over the brutal treatment of natives in the New World that gave rise to European enslavement of Africans. Bartolomé de las Casas suggested importing Africans to the Americas for use as laborers in the New World. The Portuguese arrived in Africa as early as 1441, trading first for gold, a year later for Africans. Africa became fertile ground for Christian conversion and indigenous exploitation. Thus began the European conquering of African land and natives in the name of Western Christianity. As the trade grew prosperous, other nations would enter the fray. Millions of Africans were captured, loaded on slave ships, blessed by holy men, and sold into slavery. Christian missionaries and agents moved deep into the continent—missionaries bringing the Bible and agents of slave merchants—taking the people and soon the land.

British colonies in America wrestled with the enslavement and rights of human beings. Early Europeans

direct-action program if such were deemed necessary. We readily consented, and when the hour came we lived up to our promise. So I, along with several members of my staff, am here because I was invited here. I am here because I have organizational ties here.

sailed to America for religious freedom, yet their religion (later with the exception of the Religious Society
of Friends, or Quakers) would excuse owning human
beings as chattel. In 1619, a Dutch ship anchored at
Jamestown in the mouth of the James River. The Dutch
sailors, in need of supplies, traded the Africans for food.
The colonists purchased the Africans, baptized them
and gave them Christian names. In 1667, Virginia passed
a law declaring that conversion did not change the sta
tus of a person from slave to free. Other colonies passe
similar laws during the seventeenth and early eigh
teenth centuries. In 1705, Virginia declared, "All servan
imported and brought into this Country...who we
not Christians in their native Country...shall be...slave
A Negro, mulatto and Indian slaves...shall be held
be real estate." Source: http://www.pbs.org/wgbh/a
part1/1narr3.html

Christian slaveholders saw no conflict in purch
ing human beings, baptizing them, and keeping th
enslaved. As Christians, their duty was to save th
souls, not gain their freedom. This practice strang

But more basically, I am in Birmingham because inj
is here. Just as the prophets of the eighth century B.(
their villages and carried their "thus saith the Lor
beyond the boundaries of their home towns: and just
Apostle Paul left his village of Tarsus and carried the

> reminds me of the many questions I get in my work as a Christian community developer. "What difference does it make if you get someone a home and they don't know Jesus?" Missionaries have let injustice move forward in the name of saving souls to the

of Jesus Christ to the far corners of the Greco-Roman world, so am I compelled to carry the Gospel of freedom far beyond my own hometown. Like Paul, I must constantly respond to the Macedonian call for aid.

Moreover, I am cognizant of the interrelatedness of all communities and states. I cannot sit idly by in Atlanta and not be concerned about what happens in Birmingham. Injustice anywhere is a threat to justice everywhere. We are caught in an inescapable network of mutuality, tied in a single garment of destiny. Whatever affects one directly, affects all indirectly. Never again can we afford to live with the narrow, provincial "outside agitator" idea. Anyone who lives inside the United States can never be considered an outsider anywhere within its bounds.

You deplore the demonstrations taking place in Birmingham. But your statement, I am sorry to say, fails to express a similar concern for the conditions that brought about the demonstrations. I am sure that none of you would want to rest content with the superficial kind of social analysis that deals merely with effects and does not grapple with underlying causes. It is unfortunate that demonstrations are taking place

peril of human beings. This was and continues to be a misrepresentation of the God we serve. Spirituality and humanity should not be separated. When they are separated, they leave space to misrepresent God and harm people.

in Birmingham, but it is even more unfortunate that the city's white power structure left the Negro community with no alternative.

In any nonviolent campaign there are four basic steps: collection of the facts to determine whether injustices exist; negotiation; self-purification; and direct action. We have gone through all of these steps in Birmingham. There can be no gainsaying the fact that racial injustice engulfs this community. Birmingham is probably the most thoroughly segregated city in the United States. Its ugly record of brutality is widely known. Negroes have experienced grossly unjust treatment in the courts. There have been more unsolved bombings of Negro homes and churches in Birmingham than in any other city in the nation. These are the hard, brutal facts of the case. On the basis of these conditions, Negro leaders sought to negotiate with the city fathers. But the latter consistently refused to engage in good-faith negotiation.

Then, last September, came the opportunity to talk with leaders of Birmingham's economic community. In the course of the negotiations, certain promises were made by the merchants—for example, to remove the stores' humiliating racial signs. On the basis of these promises, the Reverend Fred Shuttlesworth and the leaders of the Alabama Christian Movement for Human Rights agreed to a moratorium on all demonstrations. As the weeks and months went by, we realized that we were the victims of a broken promise. A few signs, briefly removed, returned; the others remained.

As in so many past experiences, our hopes had been blasted, and the shadow of deep disappointment settled upon us. We had no alternative except to prepare for direct action, whereby we would present our very bodies as a means of laying our case before the conscience of the local and the national community. Mindful of the difficulties involved, we decided to undertake a process of self-purification. We began a series of workshops on nonviolence, and we repeatedly asked ourselves: "Are you able to accept blows without retaliating?" "Are you able to endure the ordeal of jail?" We decided to schedule our direct-action program for the Easter season, realizing that except for Christmas, this is the main shopping period of the year. Knowing that a strong economic-withdrawal program would be the by-product of direct action, we felt that this would be the best time to bring pressure to bear on the merchants for the needed change.

Then it occurred to us that Birmingham's mayoralty election was coming up in March, and we speedily decided to postpone action until after election day. When we discovered that the Commissioner of Police Safety, Eugene "Bull" Connor, had piled up enough votes to be in the run-off, we decided again to postpone action until the day after the run-off so that the demonstrations could not be used to cloud the issues. Like many others, we waited to see Mr. Connor defeated, and to this end we endured postponement after postponement. Having aided in this community need, we felt that our direct-action program could be delayed no longer.

You may well ask: "Why direct action? Why sit-ins, marches and so forth? Isn't negotiation a better path?" You are quite right in calling for negotiation. Indeed, this is the very purpose of direct action. Nonviolent direct action seeks to create such a crisis and foster such a tension that a community which has constantly refused to negotiate is forced to confront the issue. It seeks to so dramatize the issue that it can no longer be ignored. My citing the creation of tension as part of the work of the nonviolent-resister may sound rather shocking. But I must confess that I am not afraid of the word "tension." I have earnestly opposed violent tension, but there is a type of constructive, nonviolent tension which is necessary for growth. Just as Socrates felt that it was necessary to create a tension in the mind so that individuals could rise from the bondage of myths and half-truths to the unfettered realm of creative analysis and objective appraisal, so must we see the need for nonviolent gadflies to create the kind of tension in society that will help men rise from the dark depths of prejudice and racism to the majestic heights of understanding and brotherhood.

The purpose of our direct-action program is to create a situation so crisis-packed that it will inevitably open the door to negotiation. I therefore concur with you in your call for negotiation. Too long has our beloved Southland been bogged down in a tragic effort to live in monologue rather than dialogue.

One of the basic points in your statement is that the action that I and my associates have taken in Birmingham is untimely. Some have asked: "Why didn't you give the new city administration time to act?" The only answer that I can give to this query is that the new Birmingham administration must be prodded about as much as the outgoing one, before it will act. We are sadly mistaken if we feel that the election of Albert Boutwell as mayor will bring the millennium to Birmingham. While Mr. Boutwell is a much more gentle person than Mr. Connor, they are both segregationists, dedicated to maintenance of the status quo. I have hope that Mr. Boutwell will be reasonable enough to see the futility of massive resistance to desegregation. But he will not see this without pressure from devotees of civil rights. My friends, I must say to you that we have not made a single gain in civil rights without determined legal and nonviolent pressure. Lamentably, it is an historical fact that privileged groups seldom give up their privileges voluntarily. Individuals may see the moral light and voluntarily give up their unjust posture; but, as Reinhold Niebuhr has reminded us, groups tend to be more immoral than individuals.

We know through painful experience that freedom is never voluntarily given by the oppressor; it must be demanded by the oppressed. Frankly, I have yet to engage in a direct-action campaign that was "well timed" in the view of those who have not suffered unduly from the disease of segregation. For years now I have heard the word "Wait!" It rings in the ear of every Negro with piercing familiarity. This "Wait" has almost always meant "Never." We must come to see, with one of our distinguished jurists, that "justice too long delayed is justice denied."

We have waited for more than 340 years for our constitutional and God-given rights. The nations of Asia and Africa are moving with jetlike speed toward gaining political independence, but we stiff creep at horse-and-buggy pace toward gaining a cup of coffee at a lunch counter. Perhaps it is easy for those who have never felt the stinging darts of segregation to say, "Wait." But when you have seen vicious mobs lynch your mothers and fathers at will and drown your sisters and brothers at whim; when you have seen hate-filled policemen curse, kick and even kill your black brothers and sisters; when you see the vast majority of your twenty million Negro brothers smothering in an airtight cage of poverty in the midst of an affluent society; when you suddenly find your tongue twisted and your speech stammering as you seek to explain to your six-year-old daughter why she can't go to the public amusement park that has just been advertised on television, and see tears welling up in her eyes when she is told that Funtown is closed to colored children, and see ominous clouds of inferiority beginning to form in her little mental sky, and see her beginning to distort her personality by developing an unconscious bitterness toward white people; when you have to concoct an answer for a five-year-old son who is asking: "Daddy, why do white people treat colored people so mean?"; when you take a cross-country drive and find it necessary to sleep night after night in the uncomfortable corners of your automobile because no motel will accept you; when you are humiliated day in and day out by nagging signs reading "white" and "colored"; when your first name becomes "nigger," your middle name becomes "boy" (however old you are) and your last name becomes "John," and your wife and mother are never given the respected title "Mrs."; when you are harried by day and haunted by night by the fact that you are a Negro, living constantly at tiptoe stance, never quite knowing what to expect next, and are plagued with inner fears and outer resentments; when you go forever fighting a degenerating sense of "nobodiness"—then you will understand why we find it difficult to wait. There comes a time when the cup of endurance runs over, and men are no longer willing to be plunged into the abyss of despair. I hope, sirs, you can understand our legitimate and unavoidable impatience.

You express a great deal of anxiety over our willingness to break laws. This is certainly a legitimate concern. Since we so diligently urge people to obey the Supreme Court's decision of 1954 outlawing segregation in the public schools, at first glance it may seem rather paradoxical for us consciously to break laws. One may well ask: "How can you advocate breaking some laws and obeying others?" The answer lies in the fact that there are two types of laws: just and unjust. I would be the first to advocate obeying just laws. One has not only a legal but a moral responsibility to obey just laws. Conversely, one has a moral responsibility to disobey unjust laws. I would agree with St. Augustine that "an unjust law is no law at all."

Now, what is the difference between the two? How does one determine whether a law is just or unjust? A just law is a man-made code that squares with the moral law or the law of God. An unjust law is a code that is out of harmony with the moral law. To put it in the terms of St. Thomas Aquinas: An unjust law is a human law that is not rooted in eternal law and natural law. Any law that uplifts human personality is just. Any law that degrades human personality is unjust. All segregation statutes are unjust because segregation distorts the soul and damages the personality. It gives the segregator a false sense of superiority and the segregated a false sense of inferiority. Segregation, to use the terminology of the Jewish philosopher Martin Buber, substitutes an "I-it" relationship for an "I-thou" relationship and ends up relegating persons to the status of things. Hence segregation is not only politically, economically and sociologically unsound, it is morally wrong and awful. Paul Tillich has said that sin is separation. Is not segregation an existential expression of man's tragic separation, his awful estrangement, his terrible sinfulness? Thus it is that I can urge men to obey the 1954 decision of the Supreme Court, for it is morally right; and I can urge them to disobey segregation ordinances, for they are morally wrong.

Let us consider a more concrete example of just and unjust laws. An unjust law is a code that a numerical or power majority group compels a minority group to obey but does not make binding on itself. This is difference made legal. By the same token, a just law is a code that a majority compels a minority to follow and that it is willing to follow itself. This is sameness made legal.

Let me give another explanation. A law is unjust if it is inflicted on a minority that, as a result of being denied the right to vote, had no part in enacting or devising the law. Who can say that the legislature of Alabama which set up that state's segregation laws was democratically elected? Throughout Alabama all sorts of devious methods are used to prevent Negroes from becoming registered voters, and there are some counties in which, even though Negroes constitute a majority of the population, not a single Negro is registered. Can any law enacted under such circumstances be considered democratically structured?

Sometimes a law is just on its face and unjust in its application. For instance, I have been arrested on a charge of parading without a permit. Now, there is nothing wrong in having an ordinance which requires a permit for a parade. But such an ordinance becomes unjust when it is used to maintain segregation and to deny citizens the First Amendment privilege of peaceful assembly and protest.

I hope you are able to see the distinction I am trying to point out. In no sense do I advocate evading or defying the law, as would the rabid segregationist. That would lead to anarchy. One who breaks an unjust law must do so openly, lovingly, and with a willingness to accept the penalty. I submit that an individual who breaks a law that conscience tells him is unjust, and who willingly accepts the penalty of imprisonment in order to arouse the conscience of the community over its injustice, is in reality expressing the highest respect for law.

Of course, there is nothing new about this kind of civil disobedience. It was evidenced sublimely in the refusal of Shadrach, Meshach and Abednego to obey the laws of Nebuchadnezzar, on the ground that a higher moral law was at stake. It was practiced superbly by the early Christians, who were willing to face hungry lions and the excruciating pain of chopping blocks rather than submit to certain unjust laws of the Roman Empire. To a degree, academic freedom is a reality today because Socrates practiced civil disobedience. In our own nation, the Boston Tea Party represented a massive act of civil disobedience.

We should never forget that everything Adolf Hitler did in Germany was "legal" and everything the Hungarian freedom fighters did in Hungary was "illegal." It was "illegal" to aid and comfort a Jew in Hitler's Germany. Even so, I am sure that, had I lived in Germany at the time, I would have aided and comforted my Jewish brothers. If today I lived in a Communist country where certain principles dear to the Christian faith are suppressed, I would openly advocate disobeying that country's antireligious laws.

I must make two honest confessions to you, my Christian and Jewish brothers. First, I must confess that over the past few years I have been gravely disappointed with the white moderate. I have almost reached the regrettable conclusion that the Negro's great stumbling block in his stride toward freedom is not the White Citizen's Counciler or the Ku Klux Klanner, but the white moderate, who is more devoted to "order" than to justice; who prefers a negative peace which is the absence of tension to a positive peace which is the presence of justice; who constantly says: "I agree with you in the goal you seek, but I cannot agree with your methods of direct action"; who paternalistically believes he can set the timetable for another man's freedom; who lives by a mythical concept of time and who constantly advises the Negro to wait for a "more convenient season." Shallow understanding from people of good will is more frustrating than absolute misunderstanding from people of ill will. Lukewarm acceptance is much more bewildering than outright rejection.

I had hoped that the white moderate would understand that law and order exist for the purpose of establishing justice and that when they fail in this purpose they become the dangerously structured dams that block the flow of social progress. I had hoped that the white moderate would understand that the present tension in the South is a necessary phase of the transition from an obnoxious negative peace, in which the Negro passively accepted his unjust plight, to a substantive and positive peace, in which all men will respect the dignity and worth of human personality. Actually, we who engage in nonviolent direct action are not the creators of tension. We merely bring to the surface the hidden tension that is already alive. We bring it out in the open, where it can be seen and dealt with. Like a boil that can never be cured so long as it is covered up but must be opened with all its ugliness to the natural medicines of air and light, injustice must be exposed, with all the tension its exposure creates, to the light of human conscience and the air of national opinion before it can be cured.

In your statement you assert that our actions, even though peaceful, must be condemned because they precipitate violence. But is this a logical assertion? Isn't this like condemning a robbed man because his possession of money precipitated the evil act of robbery? Isn't this like condemning Socrates because his unswerving commitment to truth and his philosophical inquiries precipitated the act by the misguided populace in which they made him drink hemlock? Isn't this like condemning Jesus because his unique God-consciousness and never-ceasing devotion to God's will precipitated the evil act of crucifixion? We must come to see that, as the federal courts have consistently affirmed, it is wrong to urge an individual to cease his efforts to gain his basic constitutional rights because the quest may precipitate violence. Society must protect the robbed and punish the robber.

I had also hoped that the white moderate would reject the myth concerning time in relation to the struggle for freedom. I have just received a letter from a white brother in Texas. He writes: "All Christians know that the colored people will receive equal rights eventually, but it is possible that you are in too great a religious hurry. It has taken Christianity almost two thousand years to accomplish what it has. The teachings of Christ take time to come to earth." Such an attitude stems from a tragic misconception of time, from the strangely rational notion that there is something in the very flow of time that will inevitably cure all ills. Actually, time itself is neutral; it can be used either destructively or constructively. More and more I feel that the people of ill will have used time much more effectively than have the people of good will. We will have to repent in this generation not merely for the hateful words and actions of the bad people but for the appalling silence of the good people. Human progress never rolls in on wheels of inevitability; it comes through the tireless efforts of men willing to be co-workers with God, and without this hard work, time itself becomes an ally of the forces of social stagnation. We must use time creatively, in the knowledge that the time is always ripe to do right. Now is the time to make real the promise of democracy and transform our pending national elegy into a creative psalm of brotherhood.

Now is the time to lift our national policy from the quicksand of racial injustice to the solid rock of human dignity.

You speak of our activity in Birmingham as extreme. At first I was rather disappointed that fellow clergymen would see my nonviolent efforts as those of an extremist. I began thinking about the fact that I stand in the middle of two opposing forces in the Negro community. One is a force of complacency, made up in part of Negroes who, as a result of long years of oppression, are so drained of self-respect and a sense of "somebodiness" that they have adjusted to segregation; and in part of a few middle class Negroes who, because of a degree of academic and economic security and because in some ways they profit by segregation, have become insensitive to the problems of the masses. The other force is one of bitterness and hatred, and it comes perilously close to advocating violence. It is expressed in the various black nationalist groups that are springing up across the nation, the largest and best-known being Elijah Muhammad's Muslim movement. Nourished by the Negro's frustration over the continued existence of racial discrimination, this movement is made up of people who have lost faith in America, who have absolutely repudiated Christianity, and who have concluded that the white man is an incorrigible "devil."

I have tried to stand between these two forces, saying that we need emulate neither the "do-nothingism" of the complacent nor the hatred and despair of the black nationalist. For there is the more excellent way of love and nonviolent protest. I am grateful to God that, through the influence of the Negro church, the way of nonviolence became an integral part of our struggle.

If this philosophy had not emerged, by now many streets of the South would, I am convinced, be flowing with blood. And I am further convinced that if our white brothers dismiss as "rabble-rousers" and "outside agitators" those of us who employ nonviolent direct action, and if they refuse to support our nonviolent efforts, millions of Negroes will, out of frustration and despair, seek solace and security in black-nationalist ideologies—a development that would inevitably lead to a frightening racial nightmare.

Oppressed people cannot remain oppressed forever. The yearning for freedom eventually manifests itself, and that is what has happened to the American Negro. Something within has reminded him of his birthright of freedom, and something without has reminded him that it can be gained. Consciously or unconsciously, he has been caught up by the Zeitgeist, and with his black brothers of Africa and his brown and yellow brothers of Asia, South America and the Caribbean, the United States Negro is moving with a sense of great urgency toward the promised land of racial justice. If one recognizes this vital urge that has engulfed the Negro community, one should readily understand why public demonstrations are taking place. The Negro has many pent-up resentments and latent frustrations, and he must release them. So let him march; let him make prayer pilgrimages to the city hall; let him go on freedom rides—and try to understand why he must do so. If his repressed emotions are not released in nonviolent ways, they will seek expression through violence; this is not a threat but a fact of history. So I have not said to my people: "Get rid of your discontent." Rather, I have tried to say that this normal and healthy discontent can be channeled into the creative outlet of nonviolent direct action. And now this approach is being termed extremist.

But though I was initially disappointed at being categorized as an extremist, as I continued to think about the matter I gradually gained a measure of satisfaction from the label. Was not Jesus an extremist for love? "Love your enemies, bless them that curse you, do good to them that hate you, and pray for them which despitefully use you, and persecute you." Was not Amos an extremist for justice? "Let justice roll down like waters and righteousness like an ever-flowing stream." Was not Paul an extremist for the Christian Gospel? "I bear in my body the marks of the Lord Jesus." Was not Martin Luther an extremist? "Here I stand; I cannot do otherwise, so help me God." And John Bunyan: "I will stay in jail to the end of my days before I make a butchery of my conscience." And Abraham Lincoln: "This nation cannot survive half slave and half free." And Thomas Jefferson: "We hold these truths to be self-evident, that all men are created equal..." So the question is not whether we will be extremists, but what kind of extremists we will be. Will we be extremists for hate or for love? Will we be extremists for the preservation of injustice or for the extension of justice? In that dramatic scene on Calvary's hill three men were crucified. We must never forget that all three were crucified for the same crime—the crime of extremism. Two were extremists for immorality, and thus fell below their environment. The other, Jesus Christ, was an extremist for love, truth and goodness, and thereby rose above his environment. Perhaps the South, the nation and the world are in dire need of creative extremists.

I had hoped that the white moderate would see this need. Perhaps I was too optimistic; perhaps I expected too much. I suppose I should have realized that few members of the oppressor race can understand the deep groans and passionate yearnings of the oppressed race, and still fewer have the vision to see that injustice must be rooted out by strong, persistent and determined action. I am thankful, however, that some of our white brothers in the South have grasped the meaning of this social revolution and committed themselves to it. They are still too few in quantity, but they are big in quality. Some—such as Ralph McGill, Lillian Smith, Harry Golden, James McBride Dabbs, Ann Braden and Sarah Patton Boyle—have written about our struggle in eloquent and prophetic terms. Others have marched with us down nameless streets of the South. They have languished in filthy, roach-infested jails, suffering the abuse and brutality of policemen who view them as "dirty nigger-lovers." Unlike so many of their moderate brothers and sisters, they have recognized the urgency of the moment and sensed the need for powerful "action" antidotes to combat the disease of segregation.

Let me take note of my other major disappointment. I have been so greatly disappointed with the white church and its leadership. Of course, there are some notable exceptions. I am not unmindful of the fact that each of you has taken some significant stands on this issue. I commend you, Reverend Stallings, for your Christian stand on this past Sunday, in welcoming Negroes to your worship service on a nonsegregated basis. I commend the Catholic leaders of this state for integrating Spring Hill College several years ago.

But despite these notable exceptions, I must honestly reiterate that I have been disappointed with the church. I do not say this as one of those negative critics who can always find something wrong with the church. I say this as a minister of the Gospel, who loves the church; who was nurtured in its bosom; who has been sustained by its spiritual blessings and who will remain true to it as long as the cord of life shall lengthen.

When I was suddenly catapulted into the leadership of the bus protest in Montgomery, Alabama, a few years ago, I felt we would be supported by the white church. I felt that the white ministers, priests and rabbis of the South would be among our strongest allies. Instead, some have been outright opponents, refusing to understand the freedom movement and misrepresenting its leaders; all too many others have been more cautious than courageous and have remained silent behind the anesthetizing security of stained-glass windows.

In spite of my shattered dreams, I came to Birmingham with the hope that the white religious leadership of this community would see the justice of our cause and, with deep moral concern, would serve as the channel through which our just grievances could reach the power structure. I had hoped that each of you would understand. But again I have been disappointed.

I have heard numerous southern religious leaders admonish their worshipers to comply with a desegregation decision because it is the law, but I have longed to hear white ministers declare: "Follow this decree because integration is morally right and because the Negro is your brother." In the midst of blatant injustices inflicted upon the Negro, I have watched white churchmen stand on the sideline and mouth pious irrelevancies and sanctimonious trivialities. In the midst of a mighty struggle to rid our nation of racial and economic injustice, I have heard many ministers say: "Those are social issues, with which the Gospel has no real concern." And I have watched many churches commit themselves to a completely otherworldly religion which makes a strange, un-Biblical distinction between body and soul, between the sacred and the secular.

I have traveled the length and breadth of Alabama, Mississippi and all the other southern states. On sweltering summer days and crisp autumn mornings I have looked at the South's beautiful churches with their lofty spires pointing heavenward. I have beheld the impressive outlines of her massive religious-education buildings. Over and over I have found myself asking: "What kind of people worship here? Who is their God? Where were their voices when the lips of Governor Barnett dripped with words of interposition and nullification? Where were they when Governor Wallace gave a clarion call for defiance and hatred? Where were their voices of support when bruised and weary Negro men and women decided to rise from the dark dungeons of complacency to the bright hills of creative protest?"

Yes, these questions are still in my mind. In deep disappointment I have wept over the laxity of the church. But be assured that my tears have been tears of love. There can be no deep disappointment where there is not deep love. Yes, I love the church. How could I do otherwise? I am in the rather unique position of being the son, the grandson and the great-grandson of preachers. Yes, I see the church as the body of Christ. But, oh! How we have blemished and scarred that body through social neglect and through fear of being nonconformists.

There was a time when the church was very powerful—in the time when the early Christians rejoiced at being deemed worthy to suffer for what they believed. In those days the church was not merely a thermometer that recorded the ideas and principles of popular opinion; it was a thermostat that transformed the mores of society. Whenever the early Christians entered a town, the people in power became disturbed and immediately sought to convict the Christians for being "disturbers of the peace" and "outside agitators." But the Christians pressed on, in the conviction that they were "a colony of heaven," called to obey God rather than man. Small in number, they were big in commitment. They were too God intoxicated to be "astronomically intimidated." By their effort and example they brought an end to such ancient evils as infanticide and gladiatorial contests.

Things are different now. So often the contemporary church is a weak, ineffectual voice with an uncertain sound. So often it is an archdefender of the status quo. Far from being disturbed by the presence of the church, the power structure of the average community is consoled by the church's silent— and often even vocal—sanction of things as they are.

But the judgment of God is upon the church as never before. If today's church does not recapture the sacrificial spirit of the early church, it will lose its authenticity, forfeit the loyalty of millions, and be dismissed as an irrelevant social club with no meaning for the twentieth century. Every day

I meet young people whose disappointment with the church has turned into outright disgust.

Perhaps I have once again been too optimistic. Is organized religion too inextricably bound to the status quo to save our nation and the world? Perhaps I must turn my faith to the inner spiritual church, the church within the church, as the true *ekklesia* and the hope of the world. But again I am thankful to God that some noble souls from the ranks of organized religion have broken loose from the paralyzing chains of conformity and joined us as active partners in the struggle for freedom. They have left their secure congregations and walked the streets of Albany, Georgia, with us. They have gone down the highways of the South on tortuous rides for freedom. Yes, they have gone to jail with us. Some have been dismissed from their churches, have lost the support of their bishops and fellow ministers. But they have acted in the faith that right defeated is stronger than evil triumphant. Their witness has been the spiritual salt that has preserved the true meaning of the Gospel in these troubled times. They have carved a tunnel of hope through the dark mountain of disappointment.

I hope the church as a whole will meet the challenge of this decisive hour. But even if the church does not come to the aid of justice, I have no despair about the future. I have no fear about the outcome of our struggle in Birmingham, even if our motives are at present misunderstood. We will reach the goal of freedom in Birmingham and all over the nation, because the goal of America is freedom. Abused and scorned though we may be, our destiny is tied up with America's destiny. Before the pilgrims landed at Plymouth, we were here. Before the pen of Jefferson etched the majestic words of the Declaration of Independence across the pages of history, we were here. For more than two centuries our forebears labored in this country without wages; they made cotton king; they built the homes of their masters while suffering gross injustice and shameful humiliation—and yet out of a bottomless vitality they continued to thrive and develop. If the inexpressible cruelties of slavery could not stop us, the opposition we now face will surely fail. We will win our freedom because the sacred heritage of our nation and the eternal will of God are embodied in our echoing demands.

Before closing I feel impelled to mention one other point in your statement that has troubled me profoundly. You warmly commended the Birmingham police force for keeping "order" and "preventing violence." I doubt that you would have so warmly commended the police force if you had seen its dogs sinking their teeth into unarmed, nonviolent Negroes. I doubt that you would so quickly commend the policemen if you were to observe their ugly and inhumane treatment of Negroes here in the city jail; if you were to watch them push and curse old Negro women and young Negro girls; if you were to see them slap and kick old Negro men and young boys; if you were to observe them, as they did on two occasions, refuse to give us food because we wanted to sing our grace together. I cannot join you in your praise of the Birmingham police department.

It is true that the police have exercised a degree of discipline in handing the demonstrators. In this sense they have conducted themselves rather "nonviolently" in public. But for what purpose? To preserve the evil system of segregation.

Over the past few years I have consistently preached that nonviolence demands that the means we use must be as pure as the ends we seek. I have tried to make clear that it is wrong to use immoral means to attain moral ends. But now I must affirm that it is just as wrong, or perhaps even more so, to use moral means to preserve immoral ends. Perhaps Mr. Connor and his policemen have been rather nonviolent in public, as was Chief Pritchett in Albany, Georgia, but they have used the moral means of nonviolence to maintain the immoral end of racial injustice. As T. S. Eliot has said: "The last temptation is the greatest treason: To do the right deed for the wrong reason."

I wish you had commended the Negro sit-inners and demonstrators of Birmingham for their sublime courage, their willingness to suffer and their amazing discipline in the midst of great provocation. One day the South will recognize its real heroes. There will be the James Merediths, with the noble sense of purpose that enables them to face jeering and hostile mobs, and with the agonizing loneliness that characterizes the life of the pioneer. There will be the old, oppressed, battered Negro women, symbolized in a seventy-two-year-old woman in Montgomery, Alabama, who rose up with a sense of dignity and with her people decided not to ride segregated buses, and who responded with ungrammatical profundity to one who inquired about her weariness: "My feets is tired, but my soul is at rest." There will be the young high school and college students, the young ministers of the Gospel and a host of their elders, courageously and nonviolently sitting in at lunch counters and willingly going to jail for conscience's sake. One day the South will know that when these disinherited children of God sat down at lunch counters, they were in reality standing up for what is best in the American dream and for the most sacred values in our Judaeo-Christian heritage, thereby bringing our nation back to those great wells of democracy which were dug deep by the founding fathers in their formulation of the Constitution and the Declaration of Independence.

Never before have I written so long a letter. I'm afraid it is much too long to take your precious time. I can assure you that it would have been much shorter if I had been writing from a comfortable desk, but what else can one do when he is alone in a narrow jail cell, other than write long letters, think long thoughts and pray long prayers?

If I have said anything in this letter that overstates the truth and indicates an unreasonable impatience, I beg you to forgive me. If I have said anything that understates the truth and indicates my having a patience that allows me to settle for anything less than brotherhood, I beg God to forgive me.

I hope this letter finds you strong in the faith. I also hope that circumstances will soon make it possible for me to meet each of you, not as an integrationist or a civil rights leader but as a fellow clergyman and a Christian brother. Let us all hope that the dark clouds of racial prejudice will soon pass away and the deep fog of misunderstanding will be lifted from our fear-drenched communities, and in some not too distant tomorrow the radiant stars of love and brotherhood will shine over our great nation with all their scintillating beauty.

Yours for the cause of Peace and Brotherhood,
Martin Luther King, Jr.

King's letter resonates with me because I am constantly asked why I mention race and culture so much in missions work. "Isn't the value of the work enough, even if it's done with flaws? Why are you always stirring the pot and making people think about race in missions leadership?" "Do you think it wise to say the things you say? It discourages those who are just trying to do good, to help others, to spread the Gospel." "Why are you involved in so many things around the country and connecting in so many places? Why don't you settle in to one place and let the other places solve their own problems?" One person put it this way: "Leroy, you can't help everyone."

King cites the prophets of the eighth century BC who left their villages and carried their "thus saith the Lord" far beyond the boundaries of their hometowns, and the apostle Paul who left his village of Tarsus and carried the Gospel of Jesus Christ to the far corners of the Greco-Roman world. While I don't begin to compare myself to King, or those early founders of the church, I too am involved in so many areas because injustice is there. That all communities and states are interrelated is truer today than when Dr. King penned this letter. We are a global community now, and the actions of one affect all. We are no longer outsiders anywhere in the world.

Some disapprove of my constant statements about race, culture, and the need to examine structures in the church and ministry to address reasons why there are so few leaders of color on boards and in executive positions. My critiques about funding and the lack of funder relationships with nonwhite leaders is met with requests to be careful, go slow, and wait. If you read King's letter, such responses will sound horribly familiar. And like him, I am disappointed that my brothers and sisters in missions fail to express a similar concern for the attitudes and institutionalized conditions that bring about all-white or mostly white leadership. To rest content with superficial social analysis that deals merely with effects and does not grapple with underlying causes is unchristian. Black, Asian, Hispanic, and Native Americans. Christians have been waiting patiently, giving systems and well-meaning white folks time and space to confront their peers in missions leadership. How much longer shall we wait? How many more young, talented, faithful people of color will have to be sacrificed? Will a next generation of young white men and women be given entrance and resources above leaders of color? I have unfortunately had to speak sternly in this book, but what is even more unfortunate is that the white power structure in missions has failed to listen to communities of color and failed to install broadly diverse leadership—not simply "one-ofs."

There can be no denying that racial injustice engulfs the missions community. Christian missions organizations are probably the most thoroughly segregated institutions in the world and their ugly record of mistreating people of color is widely known. The hard, brutal fact is that those who are not white have experienced grossly unjust treatment in missions organizations—fired, passed over for positions, authority questioned; the stories are horrific and the wounds ignored. Waiting for these conditions to ameliorate, leaders of color have sought to negotiate and often accepted positions for which they were overqualified in an effort to show good faith. They spoke for and hoped for change, only to be consistently disappointed when Christian institutions and ministries hired people of color as support staff, as a sign that they were open to multiethnicity and for photos on their brochures to show that they value diversity. These efforts, even when well-meaning, fall short of changing culture.

King said, "The judgment of God is upon the church as never before." I believe the judgment of God is upon missions if we do not immediately, fully, and radically diversify missions leadership. People of color must take on top positions in missions organizations. If not, missions will have no meaning for the twenty-first century. Survey after survey has proven King's words true—that in the fifty years since he penned his letter from that jail cell, the church has lost much of its authenticity, forfeited the loyalty of millions, and been dismissed as irrelevant. Just as disappointment with the church turned into outright disgust for many youth in King's day, disillusionment with missions has turned many inside the church today away from a radical sharing of the Gospel.

Dr. King raises self-purification as one of the four basic steps in a nonviolent campaign. In our endeavor to fix missions so they can truly achieve *Missio Dei* we must ask ourselves, "What does our self-purification look like? Are we able to accept the challenges of living without 'things'? Are we able to raise our family in the midst of financial struggle and do missions effectively and with joy?" The answer for those of color committed to urban missions is a resounding "Yes!" Many currently at work in Christian organizations struggle to make ends meet and raise support. They take positions that require them to raise support, knowing they will probably suffer because their networks don't have the wealth to support them at a level needed to maintain decent income. Missionaries of color go to fund-raising training, write grants, and visit donors, but the dollars are either not in their networks or are not given to them. They are, to echo King, accepting the blows of being overlooked and doing so without retaliating.

I am often asked the same question posed to Dr. King: "Why confrontation?" Why draw such negative attention to what is happening in missions? And I am grateful for his words and example in responding to the clergy of his day, which now guide me. The practices of prejudice and racism in missions must be confronted. Missionaries of color must *"create such a crisis and foster such a tension that...the issue...can no longer be ignored."* I want to prompt conversation and dialogue where those at the helm of missions organizations are pushed to offer real answers and held accountable for practices that separate people and thwart fulfillment of God's work.

Now is the time to act. We cannot wait any longer while whites in missions organizations fail to give witness to the suffering of people of color who work in their organizations—the consequence of an unjust funding system and the result of cultural prejudices that judge them inadequate for leadership. These red, yellow, brown, and black missionaries give their lives to the cause of justice, represent the Gospel, and care for those in under-resourced neighborhoods. They often do so despite few resources, insufficient funding, and little recognition. Their white peers are funded and given access to do the same work. I can no longer be silent and watch missionaries of color suffer as their families struggle to make ends meet while their well-funded, white peers are free to be creative. This gives the white missionary a false sense of success and the missionary of color a false sense of inferiority.

The section of Dr. King's letter that addresses the white moderate applies so much to the leadership in the Christian missions world today and to the white missions volunteer who has decided to live in an urban neighborhood but continues enjoying the spoils of being a part of the majority culture:

> Shallow understanding from people of good will is more frustrating than absolute misunderstanding from people of ill will. Lukewarm acceptance is much more bewildering than outright rejection.

Many advocates today for the poor who have moved into cities, ostensibly for missions, have fallen short when it comes to publicly speaking out against racism and injustice. The missions equivalent today of moderate whites in Dr. King's era will speak only in safe places behind the closed doors of conferences, meeting rooms, and forums. Like Dr. King, I am beginning to see these missions leaders as dangerous. They serve on their own terms, while looking like an advocate. And to some degree they are, but the comforts of the majority culture are still within their reach. Family and friends look out for their long-term care with savings, trusts, and material spoils. But these gestures of security keep them from fully joining the plight of those suffering injustice. It also hinders them from speaking out for fear of offending the status quo who want to feel good about themselves by sharing their wealth without challenging the unjust systems that have created it, along with their positions of privilege.

Dr. King was careful to name whites who wholeheartedly joined the struggle for justice and suffered. I, too, could name white folks who have moved into neighborhoods where they've seen a need and who speak boldly about the current unjust conditions of our missions and service institutions. They are few in number, but they pack a big punch.

In general, Dr. King's words express my feelings about Christian missions more eloquently than I ever could and bear repeating:

I have been so greatly disappointed with the white church and its leadership…I do not say this as one of those negative critics who can always find something wrong with the church…I say this as a minister of the Gospel, who loves the church; who was nurtured in its bosom; who has been sustained by its spiritual blessings and who will remain true to it as long as the cord of life shall lengthen…

…I felt we would be supported by the white church… Instead, some have been outright opponents…all too many others have been more cautious than courageous and have remained silent behind the anesthetizing security of stained-glass windows.

In the midst of blatant injustices…I have watched white churchmen stand on the sideline and mouth pious irrelevancies and sanctimonious trivialities. In the midst of a mighty struggle to rid our nation of racial and economic injustice, I have heard many ministers say: "Those are social issues, with which the Gospel has no real concern." And I have watched many churches commit themselves to a completely otherworldly religion which makes a strange, un-Biblical distinction between body and soul, between the sacred and the secular.

Dr. King also expresses my love for missions when he says, *"There can be no deep disappointment where there is not deep love. Yes, I love the church."* I am disappointed in white missions leadership because I love the *Missio Dei*.

"There can be no deep disappointment where there is not deep love. Yes, I love the church."

The conversation on race is getting lost in today's missions world. Michelle Alexander, in her book *The New Jim Crow* (The New Press, 2010), warns that the idea that we are past race in our society is dangerous. So many whites in urban missions tell me they are tired of talking about race. You are tired because you refuse to make the needed changes that would help resolve the problem. You are tired because you feel guilty about white privilege, but do not want to relinquish it. You are tired because the anger that comes along with the discussions frightens you. You are tired because you are weary of hearing or explaining the same thing again and again, but do not want to really change. You are tired because you feel misunderstood, that you are not like "other" whites. You are tired because you feel you have already given too much and that you should no longer have to experience the pain of talking through issues of race yet again. Funny that the least threatened by the negative outcomes of racism are the most tired.

The conversations about race must continue because Native American communities often still suffer major devastation. Latino immigration issues are polarizing and African American imprisonment rates are pandemic. Asian communities still have very little voice. Discrepancies in education, housing, job opportunities, and rates of incarceration play out along such racial lines. We can't be silent if we are to fulfill the *Missio Dei.*

The example of what Bishop Tutu and Rev. Bishop Story did with South Africa's Truth and Reconciliation Commission at the dismantling of legal apartheid may be helpful for us in urban missions. They opened up venues for people to tell their stories, no matter how atrocious they were. People were allowed to share them openly for months. They listened to those who were hurt and to those who committed the inhumane acts. Let's create space for people in missions to talk and to listen. It's important that stories from those who are hurt and from those who hurt others are shared. We cannot let racism in missions go underground when so many continue to be hurt by it every day.

Silence is the weapon of racism today, and each time we in missions don't speak up about it, we threaten the work we are called to do. Neutrality also allows those who unwittingly practice racism to remain comfortable and grow deeper into postures of entitlement and delusions of service that are actually weak responses to guilt. Christians who keep silent or attempt to hide under the cloak of neutrality cannot escape accountability for the harmful effects of systemic racism.

The progression from silence and neutrality to full participation in racism's toxic repercussions is a subtle one. Without deeply grappling with racism within missions organizations, our work can become lethal. If I do not challenge racism in the world of missions, I do not love missions.

CHAPTER 15

What Is Our Missions Dream?

"We are caught in an inescapable network of mutuality, tied in a single garment of destiny. Whatever affects one directly, affects all indirectly."

—Dr. Martin Luther King Jr., "Letter from Birmingham Jail"

I wish we didn't need missions. I wish the heart of God were playing out in our lives every day in a way that honors all people. Some say missions exist so we can tell people about Jesus, but if we lived the heart of God in our everyday lives, we wouldn't need to tell people about Jesus, people would *see* Jesus in us. There wouldn't be injustices.

Missions exist because of wrongs. Missions is a correction for what is wrong, what is not just. Missions, by definition, is the call to bring the outsider in, to let every person know that they are loved by God. That goes back to the *Missio Dei*. There is not a person God doesn't love.

Missions is living the way things should be. Missions is a way of life devoted to making justice, equality, and grace prevail in broken lives, including our own. It is making shalom reality.

What about the church? It would seem to me that the church would hold missions agencies accountable about issues of race and diversity. But sadly, the problem of racism persists within the church; therefore, the church is in no position to critique others. Missions organizations that perpetuate racism and dependency are a reflection of the church's condition.

I was raised in church and discipled in the church basement by a phenomenal teacher, Rev. Greg Johnson. He challenged me about the kingdom and taught me to respect the church and its work. With a few great exceptions—churches like Renovation Church and Community Life in Atlanta, River City in Chicago, Quest in Seattle, and The Well in Portland, working hard to achieve multiethnicity in their congregations and leadership—it is becoming harder and harder for me to watch the actions of the church today. My heart hurts around uncovered issues of race as discussions are silenced and racism runs rampant inside church walls. We do not represent the heart of God. The church today and, consequently, missions today do not measure up to what God intended. We display more of our sin and dysfunction as human beings than our love for God and each other.

> *I'm praying not only for them*
> *But also for those who will believe in me*
> *Because of them and their witness about me.*
> *The goal is for all of them to become one heart and mind—*
> *Just as you, Father, are in me and I in you,*
> *So they might be one heart and mind with us.*

Then the world might believe that you, in fact, sent me.
The same glory you gave me, I gave them,
So they'll be as unified and together as we are—
I in them and you in me.
Then they'll be mature in this oneness,
And give the godless world evidence
That you've sent me and loved them
In the same way you've loved me.

—John 17: 21–23, MSG

Jesus prayed in the garden before his death that we would be one people. We have a lot of work to do to become one heart and one mind. Locked into most churches is a designation of race or culture that separates, that shapes our view of each other and of God, leaving us isolated and divided. We are not the Church. We are, at best, thousands of small pieces that contain strands of the Church. The Church does not have walls and designations; it is people from every walk of life pursuing the Kingdom of God here on earth. The Church is one expression of God here on earth.

You were all called to travel on the same road and in the same
direction, so stay together, both outwardly and inwardly. You
have one Master, one faith, one baptism, one God and Father
of all, who rules over all, works through all, and is present in
all. Everything you are and think and do is permeated with
Oneness.

—Ephesians 4:4–6, MSG

Missions can help us get rid of the separation. By serving in new ways, with new understanding, and new attitudes, designations of race can fall away. Let's stop letting the evil parts of the past hinder our possibilities. We need no longer define activities and expressions as racial, which creates stereotypes. Labels are harmful and bring negative connotations. We must recognize our sins, confess them, and change our behavior. Racism and prejudice in all forms are evil and build walls that must be removed if we are to fulfill the *Missio Dei* and be the Church. I hope one day we will not have to say we are a multicultural church, because that would be understood.

Theology also divides the church and, therefore, missions. Our understanding of God shapes our beliefs and patterns of life. I sometimes wonder if the rational study of God misses God altogether. The study of scripture is essential, but if interpretation leads to separation, mistrust, and dogma, we are not interpreting God's word correctly. Theology has been wrong many times in the past and many apologies have been given for faulty interpretation. Remember that slavery, apartheid, and subjugation of women were once theologically acceptable and proven. Serious study of scripture makes us open to correction. Theology is not always correct and is constantly growing and changing.

The Church we all desire is one where God is the center. Missions of this Church reaches across race, culture, class, economics and centers on the life and work of Jesus. It extends God's grace:

Now God has us where he wants us, with all the time in this world and the next to shower grace and kindness upon us in Christ Jesus. Saving is all his idea, and all his work. All we do is trust him enough to let him do it. It's God's gift from start to finish! We don't play the major role. If we did, we'd probably go around bragging that we'd done the whole thing! No, we neither make nor save ourselves. God does both the making and saving. He creates each of us by Christ Jesus to join him in the work he does, the good work he has gotten ready for us to do, work we had better be doing.

—*Ephesians 2:7–10, MSG*

The Church, the true Church, understands that none of this work is because of us. We need the power of the Spirit to engage the evils of this world and even ourselves. God saved us from ourselves and put us in the position to be one church. We are God's workmanship given grace to love and serve each other.

Our call to peace puts us in missions where we can be taken advantage of, and we need to prepare to be used. This posture is vital if we are to be one church and accomplish one *Missio Dei*. Please don't get me wrong. I don't mean taken advantage of and used in a way that exploits, demeans, or neglects people. Rather, I am suggesting that we are used by the Spirit and have a posture of listening to and serving each other, thereby serving the God we love. The heart of God is to know us and empower us to accomplish his mission in the world, so we must learn to yield ourselves to each other. We have to let go of what causes division and harm to others.

I grew up in a Baptist church where dancing was not looked upon too highly, but I don't believe I can let that become a theological truth and a demand that others not dance. We all have issues like this that are not helpful when it comes to building unity—dancing, drinking, loud instruments in worship, silence, clothing, King James Version or the Message. When we look at what divides us, it can be embarrassing! Certainly these divisions don't represent the *Missio Dei* very well.

Do not repay anyone evil for evil. Be careful to do what is right in the eyes of everyone. If it is possible, as far as it depends on you, live at peace with everyone. Do not take revenge, my dear friends, but leave room for God's wrath, for it is written: "It is mine to avenge; I will repay," says the Lord.

—Romans 12:17–19, NIV

Jesus said in John 16:33 (KJV): "Be of good cheer; I have overcome the world." Dr. King said, "The universe is on the side of justice." Holding these words as truth allows life without fear as we answer our call to missions. Our lives are secure in the hands of our Creator, who watches over the world. God is taking up residence wherever welcomed. As we yield our lives, God takes over.

I choose to believe we can change missions and accomplish the *Missio Dei*. I refuse to give in to cynics and naysayers. God is at work in the universe!

Leroy Barber is an ordained Christian minister who has dedicated more than 25 years to eradicating poverty, confronting homelessness, restoring local neighborhoods, healing racism, and living what Dr. King called "the beloved community."

Leroy starts projects that shape society. In 1989, burdened by the plight of Philadelphia's homeless, he and his wife Donna founded Restoration Ministries, to serve families and children living on the streets. In 1994 he became Director of Internship Programs at Cornerstone Christian Academy. In 1997, he joined Focused Community Strategies (FCS) Urban Ministries, working with Atlanta Youth Project and was the founding Executive Director of Atlanta Youth Academies, a private elementary school providing quality Christian education for urban low-income families. Leroy helped found DOOR Atlanta, (Discovering Opportunities for Outreach and Reflection) a faith-based, six-city network for service, learning and leadership development; Community Life Church; South Atlanta Marketplace, a community-based business offering jobs, goods, and services; Community Grounds Coffee shop in Atlanta; Green My Hood, which creates jobs that help save energy and reduces the carbon footprint in urban neighborhoods; and The Voices Project, a gathering that supports faith leaders of color who are shifting cultural perceptions in the media and larger society.

Leroy is currently the Global Executive Director of Word Made

Flesh, an international organization that works among the most vulnerable of the world's poor. He serves on the boards of Mission Year, The Simple Way, The Evangelical Environmental Network (EEN), and the Christian Community Development Association (CCDA).

He is the author of three books.

- *New Neighbor: An Invitation to Join Beloved Community* (Mission Year, 2008)
- *Everyday Missions: How Ordinary People Can Change the World* (Intervarsity Press, 2012)
- *Red, Brown, Yellow, Black and White: Who's More Precious In God's Sight?* with Velma Maia Thomas (FaithWords/Hachette Book Group, 2014)

He was a contributing author of *Tending to Eden*, by Scott Sabin (Judson Press, 2010) and the groundbreaking bestseller *UnChristian: What a New Generation Thinks About Christianity and Why It Matters*, by David Kinnaman and Gabe Lyons (Baker Books, 2007).

Leroy was licensed and ordained at Mt. Zion Baptist Church where he served as Youth Director with Donna and was Associate Minister of Evangelism.

Leroy has been married to Donna for the past 29 years and together they have five children.